Don't film yourself havi.., ...

don't
film
yourself
having
sex

AND OTHER LEGAL ADVICE
TO SEE YOU THROUGH THE
AGE OF SOCIAL MEDIA

Emma Sadleir & Tamsyn de Beer

PENGUIN BOOKS

Published by Zebra Press
an imprint of Penguin Random House South Africa (Pty) Ltd
Reg. No. 1953/000441/07
The Estuaries No. 4, Oxbow Crescent, Century Avenue, Century City, 7441
PO Box 1144, Cape Town, 8000, South Africa
www.penguinrandomhouse.co.za

Penguin
Random House
South Africa

First published 2014
Reprinted 2015 (twice), 2017

5 7 9 10 8 6 4

Publication © Penguin Random House 2014
Text © Emma Sadleir and Tamsyn de Beer 2014

Text design and typesetting: Triexie Smit
Cover design: publicide

Set in 10 pt on 12.5 pt Verdana

Printed by **novus print**, a Novus Holdings company

ISBN 978-0-1435-3894-3 (print)
ISBN 978-0-1435-3142-5 (ePub)

To Miss K. The law failed you. We can only hope that this book will prevent what happened to you from happening to another.

Contents

The age of *what?*

Some important definitions

Digital age When we talk about the digital age, we mean the age of Web 2.0. It's the age of social media, digitised content and the interactive web. It's now. You're in it.

Digital native A digital native is someone who has grown up in the digital age, and who has interacted with digital technology from an early age. That two-year-old who uses an iPad better than you do? He's the quintessential digital native. So is that 19-year-old assistant you've just hired.

Facebook Facebook is a social network that allows users to build communities of friends and share content within those communities. It is generally perceived as a more private social network. It is a 'free' service, yet its founder is a 30-year-old billionaire. Fishy.

Hashtag On social media, to hashtag something is to put the '#' symbol before a word or phrase, so as to make it easier for users to search for and locate content. Overuse of hashtags is profoundly annoying.

Instagram Instagram is a smartphone application that allows users to edit photographs and videos, published to either a closed or open network of followers. Instagram is owned by Facebook.

Internet You're kidding, right? We're not going to explain to you what the Internet is. Go google it. If you then still don't know what the Internet is, or figured out that you've just used it, you've got bigger problems and we're afraid we cannot help you.

LinkedIn LinkedIn is a social network aimed at people in professional occupations, primarily used for professional networking and career-path management. LinkedIn membership is free, but there is a so-called premium service which comes at a fee.

Retweet (RT) Retweeting involves forwarding or reposting the tweet of another Twitter user. It is similar to forwarding an email to your contacts.

1

Selfie A selfie is a self-portrait taken with a smartphone, either by holding it at arm's length or photographing your reflection in a mirror, which is then typically uploaded to social media. Selfie was named the Oxford Dictionary's Word of the Year in 2013 – a fact that no doubt makes you feel really sad about the state of the world.

Social media Social media is anything that allows a conversation over the Internet. It is all those applications that bring Web 2.0 to life, and that allow us to exchange content. Social media is about uploading and downloading, sharing and connecting. Social media is Facebook, Twitter, Instagram, YouTube, Pinterest, SnapChat, Tumblr, Flickr, WordPress, Blogger, WhatsApp, BlackBerry Messenger, WeChat, and those 600 000 other websites and applications that were launched between the time this book went to print and the time you read it.

Social network A social network is a type of social media. Whereas social media is a group of web-based applications that allow us to exchange user-generated content, social networks are a specific sub-set of social media platforms that allow people to build online networks of friends and people sharing common interests. They allow for the sharing of ideas, pictures and life events. Think Facebook, Twitter and Instagram.

Twitter Twitter is a micro-blogging platform that limits posts (called \tweets')to 140 characters or less. Content published on Twitter is typically made available to the whole world. Like Facebook, Twitter is 'free'. Also with billionaire owners. Also fishy.

Web 2.0 Web 2.0 is the Internet we know today, the Internet that goes beyond boring read-only web pages, the Internet that allows two-way traffic. Not only do 'they' give us content, but we can create and upload content as well. It is the Internet of reciprocity and interactivity, and the creation and sharing of user-generated content.

WhatsApp WhatsApp is a cross-platform instant-messaging subscription service available on most smartphones, which enables users to send text messages, images, video and audio media messages. WhatsApp was recently bought by Facebook for $19 billion. Nineteen *billion* dollars. We're going to have to sell a lot of books …

YouTube YouTube is a video-sharing social media platform owned by Google, which allows users the opportunity to upload and view video content.

Does that all make sense? Remember, we're lawyers, so we don't really understand all the technology behind a lot of what we're talking about. Luckily for us, most of this stuff is more of a feeling than an actual thing. It's all a bit 'I'll know it when I see it'. Also luckily for us – and for you – this is not a book about technology. So if, for example, we've offended you by how we defined Web 2.0, please don't send us hate mail. If you want to explain it to people better, write your own book.

PART I

WELCOME TO THE DIGITAL AGE

CHAPTER I

Introduction

You live in the digital age. Computers, the Internet, social media: all these things are an inescapable fact of life for you.

Lucky you! Because living in the digital age is awesome. Google has the answer to every question, GPS means you will never get lost, Skype makes it possible for you to have a chat over a glass of wine with friends living all over the world, and your smartphone allows you to have it all at your fingertips. The digital age is incredible because it allows us to connect with the world, and share experiences, in a way that we never could have imagined.

But the digital age is also terrifying. Why? For exactly the same reason it is so wonderful. It is terrifying because it allows us to connect with the world, and share experiences, in a way that we never could have imagined.

Let's explain: before Web 2.0, the only way you could have your voice heard on a public platform was to send a letter to the editor of a newspaper. Now think about what the process of sending that letter involved: sitting down to write it; putting it in an envelope; buying a stamp; and walking to the postbox to post it. Each and every step affording you the luxury of *time* to satisfy yourself entirely that the content of the letter was not only something that you wanted to say, but something that you wanted to say publicly. Even then, it remained possible for the editor to choose not to publish your letter, because he or she thought it defamatory, abusive, otherwise inappropriate, or simply not worthy of publication. Every stage in the process conspired to a protect you from getting it wrong.

In the digital age, every single person who has an Internet connection or a smartphone has access to a public, often permanent platform, with a potential readership well beyond any newspaper. Worryingly, this access is instantaneous: there is no drafting, no thinking, no contemplating. This is access at the push of a button; access that can have the same consequences as that tedious letter to the editor.

But, really, how bad can those consequences be?

Well, this book will show that what you say and do online – and even what you retweet, share or like – has the potential (for both you and your children) to:

- ▶ land you in prison;
- ▶ see you sued and having to cough up tens of thousands, or hundreds of thousands of rands;
- ▶ seriously jeopardise your safety;
- ▶ result in the loss of your job, or expulsion from school or university;
- ▶ do significant damage to the brand and reputation of a company; and
- ▶ most importantly, do irreparable damage to your personal reputation.

Now there are two possible reactions to this … If you're older, you're probably terrified and want to go and lie under a rock and wait for it to pass. But before you do that, you should know that it's not 'going to pass'. You see, the world is not in the habit of undoing innovation. And you should also know that, without doubt, someone is going to walk past you and your rock and take a photo. They will then, of course, post that photo online. And you will then, of course, become the latest in a long line of Internet laughing stocks.

If you're young, your reaction is probably to virtually high-five all your Facebook friends and wonder how on earth your parents survived without an iPad.

Either way, you're in it. Either way, you need to carry on reading. Because as wonderful as the digital age is, getting it wrong online has the potential to get you into some very serious trouble. Every status update, every tweet, every picture, is stored in a digital dossier of your life, and has the potential to bring about life-changing legal, reputational and disciplinary consequences for you.

We're here to make sure that doesn't happen.

So why bother?

You're probably wondering whether you should even bother reading to the end, or just throw away your computer and smartphone now and be done with it.

Not so fast.

You see, this book is not intended to scare you offline. We'll admit, it *is* intended to scare you. But we want to scare you just enough to make you conscious of the risks of living your life online. We want to scare you just enough to make you stop for a second and think before you post. We want to put you in a position where you can reap the immeasurable benefits of the digital age – personal, professional, social, reputational – without compromising yourself in any way.

How we're going to do that is by setting out some important dos and don'ts of living in the digital age. Some are really obvious, while others will surprise you. We've tried to make it fun, but please remember that we *are* very nerdy lawyers, so our definition of 'fun' might not necessarily align with yours. So, yes, you might come across some boring lawyer stuff, but we promise that every word is very important in achieving the end goal of getting you through the very murky waters of the digital age in one piece, with your life and reputation intact.

What you won't come across in this book is footnotes. There are no footnotes (because we know you're not going to read them); it isn't littered with case references or sections of long and boring Acts; and there aren't any long technical explanations of the law. Mostly, this is because you haven't paid us to be your lawyers, and if this book should teach you anything, it is that there is no such thing as a free lunch. But it's also because we don't want to put you into a book coma. We actually want you to make it to the last page without giving up, tweeting about how boring it is, and googling the ending.

So you're going to have to assume that what we're saying is accurate – we promise, it is (well, at least at the time of going to print). Or pay us, and we'll tell you the same thing in legalese and in exchange for lots and lots of money. Or, if you're feeling particularly stupid, you can go and test out some of our theories and see whether or not you land up in jail/being sued/fired/changing your name. If you choose that last option, please do let us know, because we'd love to include your story as a funny anecdote in the next edition.

CHAPTER 2

If it's not on Facebook, it didn't happen

The way we communicate is changing

 Crap! Robin Hood airport is closed. You've got a week and a bit to get your shit together otherwise I'm blowing the airport sky high!!

– Paul Chambers, tweeting from an airport in the United Kingdom (January 2010)

In the aftermath of this tweet, Paul Chambers was charged with the criminal offence of sending 'a public electronic message' that was 'grossly offensive or of an indecent, obscene or menacing character'. Having lost his job, it would take a two-year legal battle, dubbed The Twitter Joke Trial, involving three guilty verdicts, three appeals, and some very hefty court bills, before his conviction was finally overturned.

Now imagine a world before social media. It is early January, it's snowing and miserable in England (shocker!), and Paul Chambers is stranded at the airport. His flight has been delayed as a result of bad weather, and he's missing out on the chance to see his girlfriend in Belfast. Understandably, he is feeling frustrated. Venting this frustration to a fellow passenger, he jokes that if the airport does not get it together, he is going to 'blow it sky high'. Perhaps he calls his girlfriend from his brand-new brick-sized cellphone and makes that same comment to her. Perhaps he simply keeps the thought to himself.

In all likelihood, in the above scenario, Paul Chambers would go on to eventually board his flight and carry on living his boring life in relative obscurity, quickly forgetting about the comment he passed in jest on that night in January.

Finding himself in this scenario in the digital age, however, Paul Chambers chose to publish his comment on Twitter. And, as we've pointed out, things did not end well for him.

What the case of Paul Chambers demonstrates so well is that the sharing of thoughts, feelings, off-the-cuff remarks, pictures and tasteless jokes is not a new phenomenon: the novelty lies in that the social conditions in which that content is published have been fundamentally altered as a result of Web 2.0 and social media. Before social media, these comments would have been made in a café or bar, around the water cooler, on a private call, behind the closed door of a home, or simply not made at all. But experience suggests that more and more people are turning to social media to broadcast this sort of content to an online network. Instead of sitting around a photo album with our family, we publish our pictures to Facebook. Instead of telling our friends about the cute heart that the waiter put on our cappuccino, we publish a picture of it on Instagram. Instead of ranting about our boss to our colleagues at a private dinner, we rant about our boss on Twitter. We document our entire lives. Or rather, we over-document our entire lives. We have been re-programmed to believe that unless it appears online, it didn't happen at all.

In addition to breeding a culture of over-sharing, Web 2.0 is arguably also breeding a culture of attention seekers. We tend to cherry-pick only the most glamorous aspects of our lives to appear online – the exotic beach holiday, the five-star lunches, the Business Lounge check-ins, the Instagram-filtered selfies taken from our very best angle – and, in a constant effort to solicit the most likes or shares, tend to push the boundary and be more risqué.

Now for those of you who didn't grow up with this technology (or at least those who haven't yet embraced it), all of this probably seems entirely foreign. You are driven to do things based on whether or not they will bring you pleasure, not by whether or not it will make your Facebook friends jealous. For you, it seems obvious to stop and think before sharing intimate details of your life online; it seems obvious that you should keep certain aspects of your life to yourself.

But if we are ever going to get to grips with the phenomenon that is social media, and understand what people are having to contend with in the digital age, we must understand that this is more than a passing fad or annoying habit, but rather a fundamental shift in the way that we, and in particular, the generation of digital natives, communicate. Social media gives everyone a voice and an opportunity to expand social partici-pation, and the exercise of that voice has now become embedded into our cultural tapestry.

The problems of context, tone and control over audience

Poor Paul Chambers and his airport tweet is a good example of how the way in which we communicate is changing in the digital age. But it also highlights some of the inherent problems with communications made over social media.

Problem 1: Social media lacks context

Taken in a vacuum, we suppose it is understandable that Paul Chambers' 'blowing the airport sky high' could be construed as threatening. But in the *context* of his day, sitting stranded at the airport desperate to see his girlfriend, read together with his stream of increasingly frustrated tweets, it is considerably less ominous.

Unfortunately for Paul, individual social media postings are ripe to be plucked from the conversation of which they form part. In doing so, all context is lost, and words and pictures have the potential to take on a whole new meaning.

Problem 2: Social media lacks tone

To the guy sitting next to Paul Chambers, having a laugh about blowing up the airport with a big smile on his face and a sarcastic chuckle, it will no doubt have been obvious that Paul was no terrorist. Yet again, in the vacuum of social media, where what you say is taken at face value, important tonal nuances are lost, and a flippant throwaway comment all of a sudden becomes something considerably more menacing, offensive and even illegal.

Problem 3: On social media, you have no control over your audience

Picture yourself at a dinner party, having had a few glasses of wine and generally having a merry ol' time. Chances are, if you say something defamatory about your boss, or threaten to blow up an airport, you're not going to get into much trouble. Similarly, if you're a kid at a birthday party and say something rude about a teacher, there's very little chance that you'll be hauled into the principal's office on Monday morning. Why? Because your words are spoken amongst friends who know you and your sense of humour, and are contained within the four corners of your surroundings. You have *control* over your audience.

As soon as you say the same thing on social media, you lose that control. Because once content exists in digital format, it has the potential to go viral (even if initially sent privately). You have no idea who will read it and whether or not they will understand the intent behind it. And that is where your fun dinner-party banter ends, and trouble begins.

This book is going to run through a whole bunch of things that you shouldn't do on social media, but much of it comes down to these three issues. So before you post something online, we want you to remember *context*, *tone* and *control over audience*, and think carefully about how what you say has the potential to be misconstrued. You'll thank us later, promise.

The psychology of online communications

It is a fact that technology affords us an opportunity to do and say things that we would probably never have the stomach to do in person. It is undeniably easier to write a *Dear John* email – or a *Dear John* text message – than to stand in front of poor John, watching his eyes well up with tears as we tell him that we're just not that into him. It is far simpler to shout down the phone at the manager of a restaurant at which we received particularly bad service, than to shout at the young waitress, seeing the fear of losing her job manifest on her face. With technology as a barrier between ourselves and the rest of the world, free from having to experience human emotion, judgement and reaction, we find the liberty to be a more open and honest version of ourselves.

Take for example Twitter user James. In 2013, James took it upon himself to send a torrent of abuse to a professional British boxer. The boxer had just lost a fight, and James thought it a good idea to let him know that he was, amongst other things, a 'waste of spunk'.

What James failed to consider when he took it upon himself to tell the professional boxer that he was a 'waste of spunk' was that the professional boxer (who basically makes a living from punching people in the head) really, really wanted to punch him in the head.

Thanks to the wonders of social media (in fact, all he had to do was ask his Twitter followers), it didn't take very long for the professional boxer to get hold of James' real name and address. With this in hand, he set off to presumably punch James in the head.

Conscious that a professional boxer was a few minutes away from punching him in the head, and no longer able to hide behind his 'anonymous' online persona, James suddenly had a change of heart and began profusely expressing his regret for any offence caused.

No surprises there.

Now what are the chances that James, finding himself face to face with a professional boxer (who, might we remind you, makes a living from punching people in the head), would tell him that he was a waste of spunk? Unlikely, right? Yet, sitting in front of his computer/with smart-phone in hand, far away from any real physical harm and finding comfort in the ostensible anonymity provided by his Twitter username, he felt perfectly safe in doing just that.

In 2013, another young British man (let's call him Paul) found himself turning to Twitter to behave in a way that he wouldn't in the real world. For years, a group of women had been campaigning for female representation on the British banknote (traditionally decked out in pictures of famous boring old white men ... and the Queen), a campaign that gained a lot of publicity and was, in the end, successful – look out for Jane Austen on a £10 banknote in 2015!

One of the women taking part in the campaign was Cambridge classicist Mary Beard. Now, for some reason, many horrible people decided that the campaign for female representation on the British banknote was a joke, and that people like Mary Beard were deserving of abuse. So one morning Paul, presumably having woken up feeling particularly stupid, decided to tweet the following to Mary Beard:

 ... retweet this you filthy old slut. I bet your vagina is disgusting. #bbcradio2 what do you think @theJeremyVine arrest me? #ROLO

Not long thereafter, someone tweeted to Mary Beard:

 Mary, if you would like to send a copy of [Paul's] tweet to his mother, Joanne, I'd be happy to give you the postal address

Paul's response?

 ... I sincerely apologise for my trolling. I was wrong and very rude. Hope this can be forgotten and forgiven xxx

You see, when faced with a real-world consequence of his online behaviour – a very angry mother – Paul wasn't so keen on standing by his abusive message. On Twitter, he felt at liberty to be rude and abusive, whereas in the real world he was probably a sweet young man who was scared of his mommy.

While good for a laugh, what James' and Paul's stories illustrate so well is that the liberating potential of technology often reveals an unfortunate fact of human nature: when given the opportunity to hide behind a veneer of anonymity, and removed from the consequences of our actions, we somehow find licence within ourselves to behave in a manner entirely contrary to what we know about acceptable social behaviour.

CHAPTER 3

Explaining some really important legal concepts

Seriously. They're very important.
Don't skip over this part ...

The cyberspace fallacy

We like to go around telling people that we are 'social media lawyers'. We reckon it makes us sound considerably more awesome than other boring types of lawyers, like corporate lawyers and tax lawyers. And it also means that we can play on Instagram and call it work.

Now the usual reaction to us telling people what we do is, 'Oh cool! What are the social media laws like? Tell us more about the cyber laws!' Our response to this is firstly to have a little chuckle, and then to feel an overwhelming sense of concern about the state of the world. Because 'cyberspace' is not a separate, imaginary jurisdiction with its own laws and rules. And thinking otherwise is the first step to getting yourself into a whole heap of trouble.

Of course, it is entirely understandable that people *think* that the online world is distinct from the offline world. When you go online, you undoubtedly feel a sense of escapism; stepping into a foreign, new and exciting digital world. It's a place where you can meet up with people in the furthest corners of the globe, be anyone you want to be, and operate free of the constraints of real life. Yet – and this is the important bit – that sense of escapism does *not* translate to the law: there is no separate set of 'social media laws' or 'cyber laws' that apply exclusively to the online world. The same laws that apply to your conduct in the real world apply to your conduct (and content) in cyberspace.

And that is the principal premise of this book. If you take one thing away from this, we want it to be that. Highlight it. Underline it. Write it down on a Post-it and stick it on your forehead.

The chain of publication

This book is littered with references to 'publication', because most of the content-based offences that are covered in the coming chapters require 'publication'. But what is 'publication'?

Publication is making content available to one other person, whether in writing, verbally or otherwise. So it doesn't make a difference whether you publish it to a WhatsApp group of five people, to your 500 friends on Facebook, or your five million followers on Twitter. You're on the hook for it all.

Where there has been publication of content, the rule in South African law is that every single person who is directly or indirectly responsible for that publication can be held legally liable for it. So imagine if we woke up one morning to find that a newspaper had published a front-page article entitled, 'DON'T FILM YOURSELF HAVING SEX IS THE WORST BOOK IN THE HISTORY OF LITERATURE. EMMA AND TAMSYN ARE JUST SPREADING LIES. AND THEY'RE DUMB BLONDES. AND THEY STOLE MY LUNCH. AND WE SHOULD ALL MEET ON SATURDAY TO FIND THEM AND PUNISH THEM FOR INFLICTING THIS UTTER GARBAGE ON US ALL.' Unsurprisingly, we would want to sue, because it is horribly defamatory and illegal. But just *who* could we sue? We could sue:

▶ the journalist who wrote the article;
▶ the editor of the newspaper who checked the article and elected to publish it;
▶ the company that owns the newspaper;
▶ the owner of the printing company that printed the newspaper;
▶ the driver of the delivery van that delivered the newspaper to the newsagent;
▶ the newsagent who made the newspaper available for sale; and/or
▶ the man on the side of the street who sold us the newspaper.

All these people are in what is referred to as 'the chain of publication', which means that each and every one of them is responsible for publishing the content of the article and can therefore be sued on account of that content. Luckily for the poor man on the side of the street, the further you get down the chain of publication, the more likely you are to be able to avail yourself of the defence of 'innocent dissemination', which is really just a defence of 'Huh? Surely you can't expect me to know about every single word of every single newspaper I sell?'

The defence of innocent dissemination was developed a long, long time ago, when pornography was banned in South Africa. The CNA chain of newsagents was selling a book that was alleged to be pornographic, and therefore illegal, and a case was brought against the store on account of them being in the chain of publication. In its defence, CNA said that it couldn't possibly be expected to know each and every word of each and every book, magazine and newspaper that it sold, and luckily for them, the court agreed: CNA had 'published' the offending material, but that publication was without fault or negligence, since the store was not in a position to know about or control the content of the material that it sold.

What this means is that, yes, we can sue the man on the side of the street who sold us that horribly illegal article, but he has a defence that he innocently disseminated it – he was not aware or had not been made aware of the content of the publication – and can therefore not be held responsible. Conversely, if he did know (or should have known) about the content, he can be held responsible for it.

Translating this to the online space, it means that every single person in the chain of publication of online content can be held liable for that content. It doesn't matter if you weren't the one who originally wrote the tweet or article, or posted the picture: if you step into the chain of publication, you step into the shoes of a publisher.

And it doesn't take much to do this: retweeting defamatory content, sharing a post on Facebook, being tagged in a status, posting a picture on Instagram, and even liking a photograph, all have the potential to be deemed an interception into the chain.

Capacity

If you're under 18 and reading this (High five! Good for you!), we bet you're thinking that you can just put the book down, tell your mother you read it, and spend the rest of the day sitting in your room playing Candy Crush.

We hate to break it to you, but you do actually need to pay attention. Not only because the reputational consequences of getting it wrong online can seriously jeopardise your future, but because you can actually get into a lot of trouble with the law, even if you're a child. More on this in Chapter 33.

Jurisdiction

Jurisdiction is just a fancy Latin word for the power or ability to make legal judgments. Putting it simply, it means that a South African who kills a South African in South Africa cannot be tried for murder by a court in, for example, Jamaica. In this scenario, only the South African courts have *jurisdiction* to hear the matter.

In the context of publication, if I live in South Africa and send a letter via post to my friend in Germany, that material is 'published' in Germany and, if the content of the letter is illegal, both the German and South African courts would have jurisdiction.

The problem with offences committed online is that it is difficult to determine which courts have jurisdiction to deal with any ensuing legal case. A South African can access Twitter, with its servers in the US, and tweet from Zimbabwe about someone in Australia, and that tweet can then be viewed in the UK, Germany, South Korea, Fiji, Brazil, Canada or any other country in the world.

What if that tweet is defamatory or otherwise illegal? Typically, the country where the content was published has jurisdiction to determine its unlawfulness. Unfortunately, in the digital age, the content has the potential to have been published in more than 200 countries worldwide. That means it has the potential to be actionable in more than 200 countries worldwide. Although the rules governing jurisdiction are intricate, and depend on additional factors such as whether the defendant has a presence or assets in a particular country, this effectively means that your one little tweet could be held to be unlawful in a country to which you have minimal ties and whose laws are nothing like the ones you know at home.

By way of example, if you in South Africa, with one million Twitter followers, only 65 of which are in England where you holiday once a year, and you tweet something defamatory about someone in India, that tweet is potentially actionable here in South Africa, in India, and even in England. Publication to one other person is sufficient to get you in trouble. On that basis, that one tweet that reached your 65 English followers was in fact 'published' in England.

Obviously these are all worst-case scenarios, but nevertheless something to bear in mind before you hop onto social media and start being controversial. Remember how we said living in the digital age is terrifying ...

Prescription

Legal claims don't last forever. Recall that mythical article about our book on the front page of the newspaper? The potential for us to sue on the basis of that article would only exist for three years from the date on which it was published. After that, the claim will have *prescribed* or expired. It's like a cheque that's gone stale.

Again, translating this to the online space, claims arising from content published online will, effectively, never prescribe. This is because it is effectively "re-published" every single day that it appears on the Internet. If it *is* ever removed (very unusual in the digital age), you would have three years to sue from the date on which it was last available.

CHAPTER 4

But wait! What about free speech?!

Freedom of expression and the balancing of rights

We know exactly what's going to happen: you're going to read this whole book, put it down and say:

> But what about my freedom of speech? I can say whatever I want! It's … like … my right!

And you would have a very good point. But you'd also be very wrong. And we blame America.

You see, the First Amendment to the Constitution of the United States, which encapsulates Americans' right to free speech, takes a largely absolutist approach to the regulation of speech, and is particularly hostile to the notion of allowing the expression of some views but prohibiting others. Basically, the USA pretty much lets you say what you want.

Blame it on the movies, or on America's general domination of … well, everything, but somehow this interpretation of the right to freedom of expression has permeated our understanding of how things work in South Africa; something that is even more striking in the context of social media and online speech.

Let's clarify: Section 16 of our Constitution provides that everyone has the right to freedom of expression, which includes the freedom to receive or impart information or ideas.

Great! Democracy is awesome.

But wait! This is not an unlimited right. The right to freedom of expression articulated in section 16 of the Constitution does not, for example, extend to propaganda for war, incitement of imminent violence, or advocacy of hatred that is based on race, ethnicity, gender or religion and that constitutes incitement to cause harm. In addition, as is the case with each of the rights in the Bill of Rights, the right to freedom of expression is subject to a general right of limitation. What this means is that the rights set out in our Constitution may be limited to the extent that the limitation is reasonable and justifiable in an open and democratic society based on human dignity, equality and freedom.

The key when talking about rights is *balance*. Where two conflicting rights come into contact, we need to balance them in a way that is reasonable and justifiable. As the age-old legal adage goes, my right to swing my fist ends where your nose begins.

And that makes sense, right? Why should your right to speak freely infringe on my right to privacy? Why should your right to speak freely infringe on my right to dignity? There is no hierarchy to our rights – they are all of equal value in the eyes of the law – and so it makes sense that the right to freedom of expression cannot trump all others.

It's not always easy to get this balance correct, and it will always depend on the particular facts at hand. But the point is that this balancing of rights is a fundamental principle underlying the Bill of Rights of our country.

So we hear you when you say, 'But what about free speech?' and we understand that it is just so much more fun to be able to say exactly what you want, to whomever you want, whenever you want ... but you can't. Sorry.

CHAPTER 5

The greatest danger of them all

You can't undo reputational harm

'It takes 20 years to build a reputation and five minutes to ruin it. If you think about that, you'll do things differently.'
– *Warren Buffett, multibillion-dollar business tycoon and philanthropist*

In the chapters that follow, we're going to tell you about all the different ways you can get into trouble on social media. Depending just how badly you get it wrong, this book is going to show you how you could:

▶ get expelled from school;
▶ get fired from your job;
▶ fork out lots and lots of money to undo the harm you caused;
▶ fork out lots and lots of money to pay your lawyers; or
▶ land up in jail.

Now we probably shouldn't be saying this, but we're going to let you in on a little secret: yes, there is a very real risk that you do something so monumentally stupid and/or illegal online that you suffer some of these pretty serious consequences. However, the practical reality is that your social media utterings do in fact have a good chance of slipping through the proverbial Internet cracks, leaving you happily unscathed and free to live your life in relative obscurity.

But before you run rampant on social media shouting, 'You can't catch me!' you should know two things. Firstly, everyone thinks they're not going to get caught until they *are* caught. As much as we would like some fresh anecdotes for the next edition of this book, we actually don't want to see any of you in jail and/or unemployed and/or broke.

More importantly, the *reputational* consequences of getting it wrong on social media have the potential to be so much more serious and life changing than any legal or disciplinary consequences could ever be. And that is because in the digital age it doesn't take five minutes to ruin your reputation, it takes five seconds. Your reputation can be ruined at the push of a button. And you'll never get it back.

We want you to read this book with that thought constantly in the back of your mind: long after you've recovered from the hefty damages you've had to pay your victim, long after you've been released from prison, long after you've recovered from the embarrassment of being fired, the spectre of your social media mistake will continue to haunt you. Every time a potential employer googles your name, up will pop endless articles about what an idiot you are. Every time you introduce yourself to someone, they'll wonder if you're *that* Joe Blogs, the one whose social media mistake was big news a few years ago. No one will ever know you for your successes, your kindness, your brain. Your name will forever be associated with the one thing you desperately want to put behind you. And because the Internet never forgets, you will be *That Guy* forever.

And no one wants to be That Guy.

PART II

THE LAW BIT

Social media's rise to (de)fame

The law of defamation

The overarching theme of this book is a reputational one: yes, what you say and do online can have potentially serious legal and disciplinary consequences, but far more concerning is the reputational harm that you may suffer. The ease with which online content can spread in the digital age only amplifies the ease with which reputations can be ruined, and once content escapes your clutches and goes viral, it's very difficult to undo the damage.

Sadly, this is not only true for content that *you* create. The content of others has even more potential to do serious damage to your reputation – it is difficult to track, difficult to rebuff, difficult to remove, and almost impossible to live down. In an age in which we are no longer afforded the luxury of forgetting, harmful, derogatory and untrue content will forever be associated with your name, dredged up every time someone types it into Google.

Luckily for those of us who quite like our good name, South Africa has a well-established law of defamation, which protects each and every person's right to an unimpaired reputation. Luckily also for those of us who quite like our good name, there are no special laws that apply to cyberspace (if you don't know what we're talking about, read the Post-it on your forehead). As such, the law of defamation applies equally to everything you say and do online and is available to vindicate any damage you may suffer as the result of someone else's harmful and derogatory posts.

The law of defamation

Defamation is the unlawful and intentional infringement of someone's reputation through the publication of content that both refers to that person and causes his or her reputation to be impaired. Individuals, companies and political parties are all able to sue for defamation, although the State and deceased people cannot.

Let's break it down:

▶ **Publication** Remember what we said at the start of this book: it doesn't matter if the content is published to five people or five million people, because 'publication' requires publication to only one other person. In the online context, the publication requirement will be met if it can be shown that the content has been viewed or accessed by anyone within South Africa (other than the person being defamed, of course).

▶ **Content** Now, you've probably heard of the concepts of 'libel' and 'slander' – undoubtedly in some or other British book or Hollywood movie. In South Africa, there is no such thing as libel and slander, because we do not distinguish between written (libellous) and spoken (slanderous) defamation. Defamatory content is defamatory content, whether it is contained in written words, spoken words, photographs, drawings or even conduct.

▶ **Reference to the plaintiff** Obviously, if content is direct in its reference, then there is no doubt that it relates to a particular person. However, content can be defamatory even if it refers *indirectly* to a person, provided that someone reading it knows who is being referred to. For example, you could defame us by referring to us by name, but you could also defame us by referring to us as 'those tall, blonde girls who wrote that *excellent* book about not filming yourself having sex'.

▶ **Defamatory meaning** It's quite a complicated two-step process that determines whether content does or does not have a defamatory meaning, but essentially something is defamatory if it damages your reputation or good name, lowers the esteem in which you are held in the minds of reasonable, right-thinking third parties, or negatively affects what people think of you. It's the kind of content that attacks a person's moral character, or exposes him or her to derision or ridicule.

So how does this all translate into the digital space?

A good example of social media defamation came in 2013, in a case that involved a series of Facebook posts made by a woman (let's call her 'The New Wife') concerning the ex-wife (let's call her 'The Ex') of her husband (let's call him 'The Husband'). Amongst the posts was an implication that The Ex was improper in allowing her teenage stepson to bath her young children. The posts did not refer to The Ex directly: the first referred to her by her first name only, and the second made no reference to her at all. The Husband was tagged in the posts by The New Wife, and took no steps to untag himself.

The posts were held by the High Court in Pretoria to be defamatory. In making this finding, Acting Judge Hiemstra held that, despite the posts not mentioning The Ex directly, there was no doubt as to whom they referred and that, in the circumstances, the posts could easily be connected to her. Even more interestingly, it was held that, although The Husband had not authored the posts, liked them or commented on them, by virtue of him knowing about them (by being tagged) and allowing his name to be coupled with that of The New Wife, he was just as responsible for the content as she was.

The Husband and The New Wife were ordered to pay R40 000 damages to The Ex, together with her legal costs.

From Ireland to New Zealand: Social media defamation around the world

▶ **Ireland** After a taxi driver posted a video on YouTube requesting users to identify an Irish 'fare dodger', a young man was incorrectly identified as the perpetrator and subjected to what was descrobed as 'the most vile, crude, obscene and generally obnoxious comments'. An Irish court required Facebook, Google, YouTube, Yahoo! and Crowdgather to ensure that all related defamatory material was permanently taken down.

▶ **England** In 2010, a man was awarded £10 000 in damages after a former friend posted an image on Facebook showing the plaintiff superimposed onto a collage of indecent images of children, tagged with his name and the name of 11 others, together with the comment, 'Ray, you like kids and you are gay so I bet you love this picture, ha ha.'

That same year, renowned historian Orlando Figes was sued for libel on account of his 'anonymous' book reviews posted on Amazon, deriding the books of his rivals while praising his own as 'a gift to us all'. The matter was settled out of court, with Figes agreeing to pay an amount of damages and issue an apology.

(Side note: If you ever come across a review of *this* book claiming that it is 'a gift to us all', it's totally legit ... *cough* ... it wasn't us ... *cough*.)

▶ **New Zealand** In 2014, former All Black rugby player Joe Karam was awarded the equivalent of more than R4 million damages on account of persistent defamatory attacks made against him by two men on both Facebook and the Counterspin website. The statements were made in relation to Karam's support of wrongly convicted murderer David Bain, and attacked numerous aspects of his reputation.

Reputation v speech: Defamation
and the freedom of expression balance

Now you may find that the above anecdotes have scared you away from saying *anything* online, but that is the last thing we want. Social media is a wonderful tool to make yourself heard, to express your opinions, and to interact with other people; it is a 21st-century mechanism for exercising your very important, and constitutionally protected, right to free speech, and we hope that you use it for just that.

In recognition of the right to free speech, and the untenable situation that would arise from allowing anyone and everyone to object to content that is remotely unfavourable or unpopular, the law of defamation has recognised a number of defences available to anyone accused of defamation. Most importantly for our purposes, you need to know that you'll be off the hook if you can show that:

▶ The main sting of the content is *true and published for the public benefit*. It is not sufficient that the content simply be true – its publication must also be in the public interest (which, of course, differs from 'interesting to the public').

▶ The defamatory remark is an expression of *comment or opinion* (as opposed to statements of fact) that:
  ▷ is honest and genuinely held;
  ▷ is based on facts that are true or substantially true;
  ▷ is not made with malice; and
  ▷ concerns a matter of public interest.

This defence allows you to be very robust in your opinions. They can be exaggerated, unbalanced, biased, extreme or prejudiced, provided that they meet the above requirements.

▶ The content is *satirical*, in that it uses wit, irony or exaggeration to mock, ridicule or criticise someone or something. As a subset of the 'fair comment' defence above, this is particularly important in the context of social media, where content is often humorous, sarcastic and littered with hyperbole. That being said, don't think that you can fall back on this defence just by proclaiming, 'Joking!'. In order to be protected, the content must still meet the four requirements of the fair comment defence – 'satire' that is driven by malice, that presents false facts as the truth or that is intended to be taken seriously, will likely still land you in hot water.

Someone has defamed me online! What do I do?

You've come across content online that you consider defamatory. Someone has, without justification, called you a thief, a liar, a racist, a paedophile or something equally damaging to your reputation. You're angry and wondering who you can hold responsible for such an affront to your good name.

The primary remedy available to you is the ability to sue the perpetrator for damages. But before you get excited about becoming a gabajillionnaire, you should know that South Africa does not have a system that allows for the issuing of damages aimed at harshly punishing the offender – *a la* the good ol' US of A – so you're likely only to get a couple of tens of thousands of rands, plus legal fees. This will typically be accompanied by an order against the offender to remove the content and/or issue an apology.

If you are aware that defamatory content is going to be published online, but has not yet been, you may also rush off to court to stop (interdict) the publication.

> Don't fancy suing? You can lay a criminal charge of *crimen injuria* against someone who has infringed your dignity. In this instance, the infringement of your dignity will have to be proven beyond a reasonable doubt.

But who are you suing?

You may recall a little thing called the 'chain of publication' (see Chapter 3): each person who publishes content to a third party is as liable for that content as the person who originally published it. In the context of online defamation, this means that the person who originally posted the defamatory content is potentially liable, as well as the administrator or editor of the particular page, the website owner, the Internet service provider (ISP), and any person who further disseminated the content, for example by liking, sharing or retweeting.

Liability of page administrators

In an interesting case heard by the South Gauteng High Court in 2012, the extent to which a Facebook page administrator can be held responsible for defamatory content appearing on his or her page was deliberated. The matter related to a property dispute that arose when the Dutch Reformed Church decided to sell a property that had been rented by Glory Divine World Ministries for several years. Having rejected Glory Divine's offer to purchase, the building was eventually sold to an Islamic academy.

When Glory Divine began lobbying against the decision on its Facebook page, the Church and one of its ministers sought an urgent interdict to stop the publication of what they claimed to be defamatory and inflammatory comments.

Although the interdict application was largely unsuccessful, Judge Satchwell did make the following interesting findings concerning posts made on Facebook:

▶ Users who post comments on a Facebook page 'are little different from persons who have attached a scrappy piece of paper to a felt notice board in a passage with a pin or stub of prestik'. They are often anonymous or difficult to trace, so it might be tricky to contact them to tell them to delete the unlawful material.

- ▶ The creator or administrator of a Facebook page, by hanging that 'felt notice board' in a public place, provides the opportunity for unlawful content to be posted on it. He is comparable to an editor of a newspaper.
- ▶ Much as 'a newspaper takes responsibility for the content of its pages', the creator or administrator of a Facebook page has an obligation to take down unlawful postings that appear on that page. He is answerable for anything that remains.

Conclusion: the administrator of a Facebook page (or any other online platform) can be held liable for content appearing on that page. It doesn't matter if it is the business page of a multinational company or the private page of a little old lady.

Liability of social media platforms and websites

In one of the leading cases on liability for online defamatory content, the High Court in the Western Cape ruled in 2013 that the Friends of Zuma Trust and Friends of Jacob Zuma website had defamed arms-deal whistleblower Richard Young. The matter related to two posts made on the website in 2008, suggesting that Young was a member of the Broederbond and a traitor, and accusing his company of being corrupt.

Young was awarded R270 000 in damages. The Court rejected the argument that the website did not have control over the posts, holding instead that it was 'not possible for the trust to sustain the pleas that it was not aware of the posting on the website given that the posts have been there in excess of five and a half years'.

On this basis, it appears as though the most decisive factor in determining whether a website host is protected from liability is the extent to which it knows of the content. This can be inferred from the extent to which the website host interferes with the content – in other words, how much it monitors, edits or deletes the comments and pictures that are posted.

In another 2013 High Court matter, an interdict was sought by H for the removal of the following Facebook comment, made by his former friend, W:

 I wonder too what happened to the person who I counted as a best friend for 15 years, and how this behaviour is justified. Remember I see the broken hearted faces of your girls every day. Should we blame the alcohol, the drugs, the church, or are they more reasons to not have to take responsibility for the consequences of your own behaviour? But mostly I wonder whether, when you look in the mirror in your drunken testosterone haze, do you still see a man?

W refused to delete the comment, despite a request from H's attorney. In response to W's submission that H should have approached Facebook to ask for the post to be removed, Judge Willis held that, notwithstanding the fact that Facebook *could* be held liable for the content, it is better for courts to focus on users, saying '... [If] one wants to stop wrongdoing, it is best to act against the wrongdoers themselves.'

This judgment has important ramifications for social media users, as it encourages those who are defamed online to sue the actual user who created the content and not the website itself.

Judge Willis went on to say:

Those who make postings about others on the social media would be well advised to remove such postings immediately upon the request of an offended party. It will seldom be worth contesting one's obligation to do so. After all, the social media is about building friendships around the world, rather than offending fellow human beings. Affirming bonds of affinity is what being "social" is all about.

Liability of ISPs

Although they are in the chain of publication, it seems a bit unfair for ISP (such as MWeb, Neotel and iBurst) to be held responsible for every single word transmitted over their network, right?

Our lawmakers thought so too, and so brought us a specially designed safe harbour. In terms of the Electronic Communications and Transactions Act 2002, for so long as an ISP does not have actual knowledge of the fact that content infringes the rights of a third party, it is not liable for hosting the unlawful content. However, as soon as such an ISP receives a takedown notification, it must act expeditiously to remove or disable access to the data.

There are palpable risks involved in this approach: even if comments are entirely lawful, by way of a strongly worded notification, they could potentially be swiftly removed. This is because it is unlikely that technological intermediaries will want to get their hands dirty – particularly when faced with threats from powerful professionals, corporations and political parties – and so will rather err on the side of caution by removing legitimate complaints, reviews and opinions without further examination. This potential snuffing out of justifiable expression clearly negatively impacts on free speech.

If someone can come up with a way to curb this obvious window for abuse, please let us know! The sad fact is that it is unlikely that website owners and ISPs will be willing to carry the risk of legal liability (basically stepping into the shoes of the person who originally posted the content) while taking the time to properly interrogate the facts and background to a particular posting, so as to make an informed decision on a takedown request.

That being said, you would be wise not to abuse the process by going around reporting anything remotely objectionable that you come across online. Because if it *does* end up in court, the chances are that a judge is not going to look favourably upon your vexatious and malicious litigation. Our guess? You'll end up with one heck of a legal bill.

Liability of retweeters, sharers and likers

By retweeting, sharing or even liking something online, you assume responsibility for its publication. If the content is in any way illegal or otherwise objectionable, you may be held liable.

The British comedian Alan Davies learned all about the perils of re-tweeting in late 2012. Following a BBC documentary about an anonymous Conservative politician involved in a child sex-abuse scandal, Davies asked on Twitter:

 Any clues who this Tory paedophile is ...?

He then retweeted a tweet that incorrectly named Lord McAlpine. A libel action was instituted and subsequently settled, with Davies agreeing to pay £15000 in damages.

In 2013, a 20-year-old Canadian woman was arrested after posting on Instagram a photograph of some graffiti depicting a police commander with a bullet through his head. There was no suggestion that she had created the graffiti. However, by publishing a picture of someone else's illegal graffiti, she had intercepted herself into the chain of publication.

Also in 2013, an appeals court in the USA ruled that clicking 'like' on Facebook is an exercise of free speech, comparable to putting up a political campaign sign in your front garden. The case related to a man who was fired for allegedly liking the Facebook page of the political opponent of his employer. Although it is uncertain whether a South African court would make the same finding when faced with a case of Facebook liking, the ruling does support a proposition that a Facebook user could be held liable for merely liking defamatory content.

So, who can I sue?

Putting the legalese aside, what does all of this mean in practical terms? What do you do if you come across defamatory content about you online? Who can you sue?

▶ You can sue the originator of the content for damages suffered on account of the harm to your reputation.
▶ You can sue anyone who shared, liked, retweeted or further dissemina-ted the content.
▶ You can sue the administrator or manager of the Facebook page, blog or other website on which the content appears. You should, however, first notify them of the content and request its removal.

As the administrator of a page or website, it is best for you to do as little monitoring of content as possible, rather requesting users to notify you of any inappropriate or illegal material that appears. If you are notified of any such content or are requested to remove it, you'd be well advised to do so. It's seldom worth the fight.

▶ You could sue Facebook, Twitter or whatever other website or social media platform is hosting the content. But don't bother. It's expensive and they will fight you with their big scary American lawyers.
▶ You could sue the ISP, but only after you have notified them of the content, requested its removal, and they have failed to act.

Help! I'm being sued for online defamation!

In the battle between the right to free speech and the equally important right to an undamaged reputation, it is often difficult to know where to draw the line. As cathartic as an online rant can be, you need to remember that the subject of your rant – be it an old flame or company from which you received particularly bad service – has a right not to have their reputation unlawfully tarnished.

We do not want to stifle the legitimate exercise of your right to freedom of expression. However, to avoid getting into trouble, here are a few rules of thumb:

▶ Be open and honest in your conduct online.
▶ Don't muzzle yourself, but be careful when walking the line between free speech and bringing harm to someone's reputation.
▶ Only comment on, share, retweet or like content of which you have first-hand knowledge and that you know is true.
▶ When you're expressing an opinion, make sure it is not framed as a statement of fact.
▶ Know that you will have to stand by your online statements by asserting one of the defences outlined in this chapter, and be able to prove that you met all the requirements.

If the horse has already bolted and you've found yourself in hot water, the best thing to do is to take down the offending post and offer an apology. If you're lucky, your victim is feeling forgiving and/or doesn't have the time or money for a long legal battle, the whole saga will be forgotten.

A final word

The law of defamation has traditionally been the terrain of 'The Media', with battles fought between well-heeled press organisations and those interesting enough to end up on the wrong side of their reportage. But in the digital age, we are all able to instantly publish content to a wide audience; we are all, in fact, The Media. The standards of the law of defamation have therefore been transferred to social media platforms and are now becoming a reality for every owner of a laptop, tablet or smartphone.

Whether or not it is correct that principles developed in the context of the press are applied equally to everyday Internet folk is certainly up for

31

debate. In our view, the law needs to develop in order to keep up with technological innovation.

Some of the most expensive social media blunders of all time

▶ In 2010, former Indian Premier League chairman Lalit Modi tweeted that the reason New Zealand cricketer Chris Cairns had been removed from the IPL auction list was because of his alleged involvement in match-fixing. Modi was ordered by a UK court to pay £90 000 damages plus legal costs (around £1.5 million).
Total damage: ±R16.5 million

▶ Caught up in the same scandal as British comedian Alan Davies, Sally Bercow (wife of the Speaker of the House of Commons) was ordered to pay damages to Lord McAlpine after tweeting in the aftermath of the BBC allegations, 'Why is McAlpine trending? *innocent face*.' The tweet was held to be defamatory, in that it implied that Lord McAlpine was a paedophile. Together with legal fees, the tweet is reported to have cost Bercow around £100 000.
Total damage: ±R1.7 million (that's more than R45 000 per letter ...)

▶ Also in the UK, after an independent commission set up by the Football Association (FA) cast doubt on Chelsea player Ashley Cole's evidence in a case of racial abuse brought against his teammate John Terry in 2012, Cole tweeted, 'Hahahahaa, well done #fa I lied did I, #BUNCHOFTWATS.' His tweet was retweeted over 19 000 times before being deleted. He was fined £90 000 by the FA.
Total damage: ±R1.5 million (but before you start feeling too sorry for him, you should know that that's only about half his weekly earnings)

▶ In Australia, a 20-year-old man who published a series of defamatory Facebook posts and tweets about a music teacher at his former school was ordered to pay AUS$105 000 in damages to his victim. In his judgment, Judge Michael Elkaim said that the evil of defamatory publications on social media 'lies in the grapevine effect that stems from the use of this type of communication'.
Total damage: ±R1 million

▶ In Florida, long-standing headmaster Patrick Snay sued Gulliver Schools for age discrimination when they failed to renew his employment contract. In 2011, the parties reached a settlement agreement, which included a non-disclosure provision requiring the existence and terms of the agreement to be kept confidential. A few days later, Snay's daughter posted on Facebook, 'Mama and Papa Snay won the case against Gulliver. Gulliver is now officially paying for my vacation to Europe this summer. SUCK IT.' The Florida Court of Appeal found that Snay had breached the agreement with Gulliver and revoked the $80 000 settlement. We're guessing that European vacation was swiftly cancelled by Mama and Papa Snay ...

Total damage: ±R830 000

The most expensive reaction to an Instagram photo ...

On 25 April 2014, audio was released of Donald Sterling – owner of the Los Angeles (LA) Clippers basketball franchise – ranting at his girlfriend V Stiviano about how he does not want her to bring black people to his games. The argument stemmed from an Instagram picture posted by Stiviano, which showed her posing with NBA legend Magic Johnson. Included in Sterling's racist diatribe:

▶ 'It bothers me a lot that you want to broadcast that you're associating with black people. Do you have to?'
▶ 'You can sleep with [black people]. You can bring them in, you can do whatever you want. The little I ask you is not to promote it on that ... and not to bring them to my games.'
▶ 'I'm just saying, in your lousy fucking Instagrams, you don't have to have yourself with, walking with black people.'

Following the remarks being made public, LA Clippers' sponsors Chumash Casino, CarMax, Virgin America and Kia Motors terminated their relationship with the team. Sterling was subsequently banned from the National Basketball Association (NBA) for life and fined $2.5 million (± R26 million). The NBA also took steps to force Sterling to sell the LA Clippers franchise, which is estimated to be worth $500 million (over R5 billion).

CHAPTER 7

Is privacy dead?

Big data, surveillance and the law of privacy

'Privacy is dead. Get over it.'
– *Steve Rambam (2006)*

Mapping your digital footprint: The big data revolution

The Internet is an extraordinary thing. It gives us access to information beyond our wildest dreams; let's us connect with anyone and everyone; and gives us the ability to do things that we didn't even know we wanted to do in the first place. Social networks, blogs, online games, news websites, instant messaging, discussion forums, webmail, apps and online navigation tools have become such an integral part of everyday life that they are almost impossible to live without.

And the best part is that it's all for *free* (yippee!).

But wait? If it's for *free* (yippee?), why are the companies and people that run these websites, platforms and online tools worth billions and billions of dollars?

Well, they're worth billions and billions of dollars because these online services are *not* free. You pay for each and every one of them with the most valuable thing you own – something more valuable than money: your personal information.

This sounds terribly alarmist, we know, but the websites and mobile apps that you use owe you *nothing.* To them, you're a vessel of personal data, to be mined to the fullest extent possible. Every time you go online and post/buy/like/play/view/share/upload/download/send something, you add one more dot of colour to the picture that online companies are painting of you, to be sold to the highest bidder.

▶ You just updated your relationship status to 'Engaged' on your private Facebook page? *Get ready to be bombarded with adverts about wedding venues.*
▶ You searched for a flight to London? *Cue the ads for hotels and car rentals.*
▶ You liked a picture of a puppy? *Dogfood promotions are coming your way.*

- Bought a new jacket online? *You'll need some shoes to go with that. And a new handbag.*
- You sent someone an email about how your new flowerbeds are blossoming in the sunshine. *Obviously you need a lawnmower.*

> In late 2013, Google launched 'shared endorsements'. Aimed at 'ensuring that your recommendations reach the people you care about', Google may now 'display your reviews, recommendations and other relevant activity throughout its products and services', together with your profile name and photo. You can opt out of shared endorsements via your Google account settings.

*Insight into that Privacy Policy that we know you didn't read ...**

When you set up your various social media accounts, you ticked a box that confirmed that you had read the site's Privacy Policy. But we bet you didn't ... so we've summarised some of the important ones for you.

- **Facebook** uses the information it receives about you to, amongst other things, provide location features, deliver relevant ads, make suggestions to you, and provide other innovative yet-to-be-developed services that use the information in new ways. This information includes your registration information, birthday, status updates, photos (including the time, date and place you took the photo), comments, likes, place tags, relationship status, IP address, location, as well as details about when you log on, when you look at someone's timeline, when you receive a message, and when you search for someone. That's rather a lot of information!

- **Instagram** uses the information it collects to, amongst other things, provide personalised content and marketing, and may share such information with third-party advertisers. This information includes your registration information, profile information, photos, comments, hashtags, geotags, IP address and device type.

- **LinkedIn** uses information including your registration information, job title, education, professional experience, groups, imported contacts, which ads you click on, mobile carrier, your location and IP address, as well as information inferred from your profile (for example, using job titles to infer age, seniority and compensation bracket) to provide customised content. This information may also be shared with the administrators of pages that you follow.

*As of May 2014. These policies may, of course, change at any time.

Basically, they have rights to do a lot of stuff with the information you give them.

Now, if you have extreme levels of paranoia, your reaction to this will be to delete all your online accounts and go live under that rock that we spoke about right in the beginning. If you're a realist, your reaction will be to resign yourself to the fact that we live in an age in which big data is king and accept that it is the quid pro quo of getting cool stuff for 'free'. You'll decide that you actually don't mind that Facebook has a digital file on you that could tell you things about yourself that even you didn't know and that this file is being sold on to advertising companies, as long as you don't have to pay for their services (with money). How else are you going to Facebook-stalk your ex and judge people for posting pictures of their uterus online? And, hey, maybe it'll be useful if you lose your keys, since Google probably knows where they are.

What we would advocate is a reaction somewhere in between the two. The platforms are great and have a lot of value, so there really isn't a need to panic. But, also, just be conscious of the digital dossier that you're busy populating with every intricate detail of your life. Ultimately, feel empowered. Because now at least you *know* that they *know* all about you, so you can give the Google Maps car a smile and a wave as it drives past your house.

Keeping a low (Facebook) profile

'When we got started just in my dorm room at Harvard, the question a lot of people asked was "Why would I want to put any information on the Internet at all? Why would I want to have a website?" And then in the last 5 or 6 years, blogging has taken off in a huge way and all these different services that have people sharing all this information. People have really gotten comfortable not only sharing more information and different kinds, but more openly and with more people. And that social norm is just something that has evolved over time.'
– *Mark Zuckerberg, Facebook CEO, TechCrunch Interview at The Crunchies (2010)*

There are a few standard reactions to people getting into trouble for what they say and do online:

▶ 'It wasn't me. My friend stole my phone.'
▶ 'I was joking. Lol.'
▶ 'It was on my private page.'

Unfortunately for those who resort to Option 1, the 'it wasn't me' excuse is getting a bit tired, and you will still have to prove that you were not in fact responsible for publishing the offending content. Unfortunately for those who resort to Option 3, in a world where privacy is perhaps no longer a social norm, and where traditionally 'private' facts are routinely documented and shared, it becomes infinitely more difficult to distinguish between private and public spaces. Is there really such a thing as privacy online?

In South Africa, the right to privacy is recognised in the Constitution and protected in terms of a number of statutory provisions as well as the common law of privacy. Simply put, the law protects information over which someone can be said to have a 'legitimate expectation of privacy'. If, in the given circumstances, you legitimately and reasonably expect that particular facts will be kept private, then those facts are protected from intrusion and disclosure.

This right is, however, not absolute, and may in some instances be out-weighed by a conflicting right, for example, someone else's right to free-dom of expression. There are also certain defences available that allow for the lawful disclosure of private facts. Most importantly, your privacy will not be infringed when:

▶ you gave your informed and voluntary *consent* to the access or dis-closure of your private information (for example, when you have public-ly said that you are homosexual); or
▶ the access or disclosure of the information was in the *public interest* (for example, because it exposed immoral, illegal or hypocritical behaviour).

'A legitimate expectation of privacy'

So when can you be said to have a legitimate expectation of privacy in respect of information that you post online? Well, the first step is to determine whether or not the information is inherently private.

Certain information, by its very nature, warrants an expectation of privacy, while other information does not. As the Constitutional Court said in *Investigating Directorate: Serious Economic Offences and Others v Hyundai Motor Distributors (Pty) Ltd and Others; In Re Hyundai Motor Distributors (Pty) Ltd and Others v Smit NO and Others* (potentially the longest case name in the history of case names):

> privacy is a right which becomes more intense the closer it moves to the intimate personal sphere of life of human beings, and less intense as it moves away from that core.

So the more intimate the information, the more private it is.

This is not altered by the fact that the information is accessed via social media. Just as is the case offline, intimate information about a person's health, finances, body, emotional distress, political opinions, past criminal involvement and private correspondence will all attract an expectation of privacy in the social media environment. For example, your HIV status is intrinsically private whether it is hidden in a file in a doctor's office or posted online. Naked pictures of yourself are intrinsically private whether stored in a shoebox at the back of your cupboard or posted online.

The novelty of social media is not that it changes the inherently private nature of information, but rather that it places the *legitimacy* of the expectation of privacy in respect of that information in a new light.

It's all a bit technical and lawyerly, we know. Essentially, what we mean is that inherently private information remains private information, whether posted on social media or not. But in a world in which we voluntarily elect to share traditionally 'private' information on public platforms, we need to ask whether we can *legitimately* expect that that information remains private.

We think there are a few factors that may be relevant to making this determination.

1. Just how private is the platform on which it is shared?

It is possible to draw a distinction between open and closed social media platforms. Although most websites allow for privacy settings to be tailored, there is no doubt that sites such as Twitter, YouTube and blogs adopt an open system, designed to disseminate information as widely as possible (rather like a newspaper). Websites such as Facebook and LinkedIn, on the other hand, operate a semi-closed model, with only those who have been accepted into a limited network of connections able to view published content (like being part of a closed circle of friends). In our view, information published on an open social media platform warrants a lower expectation of privacy than that posted on a closed social media platform.

In addition, irrespective of the intrinsic nature of the platform, the privacy settings invoked by an individual should also be considered a matter of enormous significance. If a user has, for example, elected by way of negligible privacy settings to open up an inherently closed network such as Facebook, so that all information posted on the site is available to the wider public, this should act to lower a claim to privacy. Similarly, if you choose to close an inherently open network such as Instagram or Twitter, you should have a stronger claim that the information is private. In other words:

More privacy settings invoked = Greater expectation of privacy
Less privacy settings invoked = Lower expectation of privacy

In practical terms, what this all means is that the further publication of information that was made available on an open-to-all Twitter account will not necessarily be a violation of your privacy. If, however, you have invoked full Facebook privacy settings, publication of content beyond your circle of Facebook friends could be construed as an infringement of your privacy. If someone tweets a screenshot of a conversation that took place within a WhatsApp group, that too could be construed as an infringement of your privacy.

Of course, once the cat is out the bag, you could still face serious legal, disciplinary and reputational consequences on the basis of the now-public content, but you would nevertheless be able to sue the person who disseminated the content outside of your closed network for infringement of your right to privacy.

2. Are you a public figure?

The extent to which someone is a public figure – whether by virtue of the fact that they are a celebrity, a sportsperson, a politician or simply courting publicity – may lower their claim to a legitimate expectation of privacy when it comes to certain personal facts or photographs. This is particularly true where such facts or photographs reveal some element of hypocrisy (for example, if a celebrity has publicly denounced drug use, but is snapped snorting cocaine).

As stated by the Supreme Court of Appeal in the 2005 case of *Mogale v Seima*:

> [Persons] who move in or close to the limelight have to expect that their lives will be to some extent in the public domain and they must be prepared to endure somewhat more than the ordinary citizen.

Of course, those who live in or actively seek out the spotlight of publicity still have rights, and are not automatically deprived of the protection of privacy accorded to the rest of us. However, as so delightfully put by Judge Willis in his 2012 High Court judgment in *Buthelezi v BDFM Publishers*:

> As the Afrikaans proverb goes, "Die hoogste bome kry die meeste wind." This may be somewhat inelegantly translated into English as "The taller the tree, the more it is buffeted by the wind".

The fact that taller trees are more buffeted by the wind is made all the more compelling in the age of social media where, in many ways, we are all public figures. There is certainly an argument that someone who posts endless selfies-in-bikinis and takes to Twitter on an hourly basis to disclose intimate details of his or her life has a lower expectation of privacy than someone who uses social media in a much more reserved manner.

In the end, we think that you construct your own privacy rights in the digital age. Therefore, before making content available online – on whatever platform – ask yourself whether you have an expectation that the content remains within the boundaries of the platform on which it is posted. If you do, either don't post it online, or try to bolster your claims to a legitimate expectation of privacy by taking the following steps:

▶ Don't put it on Twitter, YouTube, a blog or any other widely accessible platform.
▶ Activate as many privacy settings as you can muster.
▶ Think about how what you disclose now could affect your privacy claims in respect of what you disclose later. If you want your privacy to be respected in one aspect of your life, you'll have to guard it in all aspects of your life.
▶ Try to make your content as obscure as possible. Don't attempt to bring it to a wider audience, for example by mentioning another Twitter user, sharing it across platforms or tagging a Facebook profile.

Edward 'Ned' RocknRoll

Allow us to tell you a story about a guy called Edward 'Ned' RocknRoll (yes, folks, that's his real name) ... In the UK in 2010, Ned RocknRoll went to a 21st birthday party where (presumably) he got up to some shenanigans. Unsurprisingly, photographs were taken at this party, some of which showed Ned partially naked. And because this 21st birthday party took place in the 21st century, those photographs ended up on the Facebook page of one Mr Pope (yes, folks, that's also his real name). The photographs could be viewed by Mr Pope's approximately 1500 friends, but not by the general public.

In December 2012, Ned RocknRoll found himself thrust into the media spotlight when he married the actress Kate Winslet. A month later, the photographs came to the attention of *The Sun* newspaper (Mr Pope alleges that this was due to Facebook changing their privacy settings), which sought to publish them. Naturally, Ned rushed off to court to stop this from happening.

Granting his request to prevent the newspaper from publishing the pictures, the High Court found that Ned *did* have a reasonable expectation of privacy in respect of the photographs and their content. The Court reasoned as follows:

▶ The photographs showed Ned in the company of his family and friends at a private party on private premises, and behaving in a manner in which he would be unlikely to behave in public.
▶ It is unlikely that it could be established that either Ned or Mr Pope anticipated that the photographs would be published in a national newspaper.
▶ Ned had become something of a public figure as a result of his relationship with and marriage to Kate Winslet, but he was not a celebrity in his own right.
▶ There had been no widespread public inspection of Mr Pope's Facebook albums.
▶ There was no public interest in publishing the photographs.

Victory for RocknRoll!

What to do if you feel your online privacy will be or has been violated

To recap, the test for whether your privacy has been or will be infringed is whether you, in those circumstances, have a legitimate expectation that the content will be kept private. If so, any right to have content kept private can be overridden by (1) your consent to its further publication or dissemination, or (2) the legitimate interest of the public in being informed about the content.

If you suspect that your privacy is about to be infringed, you can apply to the court to stop the publication of private facts. However, the court will not restrain publication if the content is already in the public domain, even if that content violates your privacy.

The former president of the governing body of Formula 1 found this out the hard way in 2008, when the High Court of England and Wales refused his application for an interdict against the publication of photographs by the *News of the World*. The photographs were stills from a video of a sex orgy between him and five prostitutes – a video that was already widely available online. The court reasoned as follows:

> [I]t has entered the public domain to the extent that there is, in practical terms, no longer anything which the law can protect. The dam has effectively burst. I have, with some reluctance, come to the conclusion that although this material is intrusive and demeaning, and despite the fact that there is no legitimate public interest in its further publi-cation, the granting of an order against [the News of the World] at the present juncture would merely be a futile gesture. Anyone who wishes to access the footage can easily do so, and there is no point in barring the News of the World from showing what is already available.

So if the content that violates your privacy has already been published, you can sue for damages; however, you will probably not succeed in having it deleted.

But before you rush off to court, think about Barbra Streisand. In 2003, Streisand instituted a $50 million lawsuit against a photographer and the website Pictopia.com for violation of her privacy. The claim arose from an aerial photograph of Streisand's house in Malibu, one of 12 000 publicly available photographs of the California coastline which had been taken to document the effects of coastal erosion. Before filing her lawsuit, the picture of Streisand's home had been downloaded a total of six times (twice by her lawyers). In the month following her lawsuit, over 430 000 people visited the website. This is what is now known as the Streisand Effect – a phenomenon whereby content is widely publicised in response to attempts to have it censored.

And so, particularly in privacy cases, rushing off to court is not always the best thing to do, as it often places a big shiny spotlight on content that you're trying to hide. Take for example *The Spear*, an artwork that depicts Jacob Zuma with his genitals exposed. In 2012, the painting had happily been hanging in the Goodman Gallery for seven days, where it had been viewed by a very limited audience. However, as soon as the ANC released a statement saying that they were going to launch urgent legal action to get the artwork removed, it became headline news around the world. In attempting to have it taken down, the ANC had inadvertently dragged it out into the open for the world to ogle at.

The same is true for content online. We know you think your Facebook musings are really profound or that your blog is going to change the world, but sometimes it's only your mom who cares. If your content is disseminated beyond the boundaries of your legitimate expectation of privacy, by screaming and shouting and rushing off to court you run the risk of bringing it to the attention of a much wider audience than would have seen it if you had just bitten the bullet.

Hacking away at privacy: Unlawful interception into private spaces

We've established that:

▶ Web companies owe you nothing. They're gathering information on you as we speak.
▶ The digital age and social media have blurred the line between public and private. You should therefore never consider the information you post online as private.

As everything is stored digitally, it is also that much easier in the digital age for material to be accessed or disclosed using surreptitious means: hacking into social-networking profiles, using email or social media account login information without permission, or befriending someone using a fake profile in order to gain access to their inner network.

Our law prohibits that sort of conduct. Not only would it amount to a breach of the right to privacy, but it could potentially also amount to fraud or an offence in terms of section 86 of the Electronic Communications and Transactions Act 2002. This Act provides that any person who intentionally accesses or intercepts data without authority or permission to do so is guilty of an offence and liable to a fine or imprisonment for up to one year. The Regulation of Interception of Communications and Provision of Communication-Related Information Act 2002 (RICA) further prohibits the intentional interception of communications, unless:

▶ the person intercepting the communication is a party to it, for example the sender or one of the recipients;
▶ the communication is intercepted by a law-enforcement officer who has reasonable grounds to believe, for example, that a serious offence has been or will be committed, that serious bodily harm may ensue or that the interception is necessary in order to determine the location of an emergency;
▶ the interception is done with the consent of a party to the communication; or
▶ the interception is done in connection with the carrying on of business (see Chapter 27).

We should note, however, that information obtained illegally may still be able to be lawfully published if such publication is in the public interest – you've committed a crime in accessing it (and may be prosecuted), but a defence exists to a claim that the publication amounts to a breach of the subject's right to privacy.

Big Brother is watching: Government surveillance in the digital age

In June 2013, following a leak by former CIA and US National Security Agency (NSA) employee Edward Snowden, newspapers – including *The Guardian* (UK), *The Washington Post* (USA) and *Der Spiegel* (Germany) – published details of a treasure trove of classified intelligence files from around the world. Although Snowden went on to be charged with espionage and, as of May 2014, is languishing somewhere in Russia (having been granted temporary asylum), the damage had been done. The leaked documents detailed the existence of various global surveillance programs in terms of which the communications of citizens were being monitored by the US government, including the NSA's electronic data-mining program PRISM (which collected Internet communications disclosed on demand by companies such as Google) and a British program that monitored Twitter, YouTube views and Facebook likes.

The incident shed light on the phenomenon of mass global surveillance by governments – so easy in an age in which everything is digitised – and the need to balance the needs of State security with the informational privacy of citizens.

People were outraged. But really, in a world where we freely make our personal information available to private corporations to be used for their commercial gain, and agree to one-sided 'privacy policies' in terms of which social media organisations can gather hoards of data about us, can we really complain about our personal information being monitored by the State? And in a world where almost every day we take to social media to share intimate details of our lives with our 'friends', can we really complain that the government takes a peek?

Well, yes. Yes, we can. Because it's creepy.

For example, in early January 2014, the Ukrainian police force sent a text to thousands of protesters in Kiev reading, 'Dear subscriber, you are registered as a participant in a mass disturbance.' The text came shortly after a new law was passed prohibiting public demonstrations. The *New York Times* reported that the government had used technology to pinpoint the locations of cellphones in use near clashes between riot police officers and protesters.

Super creepy.

But it does show that, as technology gets more advanced and we become more connected to (and dependent on) digital devices, governments are inevitably turning to technology to garner information about us.

Now you might think all of this is just a classic case of First World Problems – something for Barack Obama and David Cameron to squabble over. But, just like in the US and Europe, South Africa has a (complicated) framework of legislation that allows for the surveillance of communications. Our information is equally digitised, and our government is equally capable of monitoring our communications, both lawfully and unlawfully.

Are we saying that your Skype conversations, cellphone calls, Google searches and Facebook likes are being monitored by the State? No. Are we saying that they *could* be? Yes.

Tips for protecting your (and others') privacy online

▶ Don't treat anything you put online as private. If you want to keep it private, write it in a diary that you keep under your bed.

▶ Be smart about passwords – don't use the same password across all accounts, change them every so often, and never disclose them to anyone.

▶ Be wary of geolocating. No one needs to know exactly where you are (except Google Maps!).

▶ Activate the maximum privacy settings possible (barring Twitter, YouTube and other blogging platforms, which we accept are inherently public).

▶ Be considerate about the private information that you post about other people. If they want to tell people that they're engaged/sick/broke/voting for the ANC, they'll do so themselves.

CHAPTER 8

Privacy coming into bloom

The Protection of Personal Information Act 2013

The digital age, and the concomitant digitisation of information, has seen a monumental increase in the amount of personal information being processed on a daily basis. Not only is more and more information being generated, but it is easier and cheaper than ever before to store, access, edit and distribute.

In recognition of the value that personal data holds in the digital age, and the associated need to protect the so-called 'informational privacy' of individuals, you're about to get a whole new layer of privacy protection. All thanks to the Protection of Personal Information Act 2013.

The Act was signed into law in November 2013. The cool kids like to call it POPI, but don't be fooled by its pretty flowery name: POPI is to be taken very seriously. It will bring about wholesale changes to the way in which companies and individuals manage, store and process your personal information, and gives you some really powerful rights against them if they do so in a way that doesn't comply with the law.

What exactly is POPI trying to regulate?

POPI governs the processing of personal information. We promised you we wouldn't bore you with long extracts from Acts, so we won't ... but, basically, personal information is information that relates to a living individual or existing juristic person.

▶ Your name
▶ Your gender
▶ Pictures of you
▶ The fact that you speak three languages
▶ The fact that you have the flu
▶ The fact that you worked at McDonald's when you were 17
▶ Your Twitter handle
▶ The fact that you prefer chicken to fish
▶ The fact that your high-school teacher thinks you were an annoying brat

All of the above is considered 'personal information'.

'Processing' is essentially anything that anyone does with that information. Collecting it, organising it, reading it, modifying it, linking to it, retrieving it from a file and even deleting it all constitute the processing of personal information.

So you can see how far reaching POPI is.

Go ahead, we dare you to try to think of any dealing with any kind of information that will not fail to be regulated under POPI. It's virtually impossible.

What does POPI require of those who process personal information?

Once it has been established that personal information is being processed within the contemplation of POPI, the Act imposes considerable burdens on the person or company responsible for that processing – primarily an obligation to process that personal information lawfully. It's a 76-page Act, so if you really want to read all about what lawful processing entails, please go ahead. There are also loads of books and websites dedicated solely to POPI that don't make any mention of sordid things like filming yourself having sex.

We do, however, think that you need to know the basic premise of POPI, which is that, in order for it to be considered *lawful*, the processing of personal information needs to comply with the following eight principles:

▶ **Accountability** The person responsible for processing personal information is responsible for compliance with the Act.

▶ **Processing limitation** Personal information may only be processed with consent, or if the processing is otherwise justified (for example, it is necessary for the performance of a contract). The purpose for which personal information is processed must also be adequate, relevant and not excessive.

> Think about whether the personal information you collect is relevant to the purpose for which it is being collected. The following may all be considered to be irrelevant:
>
> ▶ the marital status of someone applying for car insurance;
> ▶ full details of a medical condition or illness to justify sick leave;
> ▶ full name, address and date of birth in order to enter a public pool;
> ▶ the photograph of a patient seeking infertility treatment.

▶ **Purpose specification** Personal information must be collected for a specific, explicitly defined and lawful purpose related to a function or activity of the party processing it.

▶ **Further processing limitation** The further processing of personal information must be compatible with the purpose of its original collection. For example, if it was collected in order to process your entry into a competition, it cannot be used to market related products to you.

▶ **Information quality** Personal information must be complete, accurate, not misleading and must be kept updated.

▶ **Openness** Persons must be kept informed of when and for what purpose their personal information is being collected and processed.

▶ **Security safeguards** Steps must be taken to secure the integrity, confidentiality and security of personal information.

▶ **Data subject participation** Those whose personal information is processed have various rights in relation to such processing.

All very legal-y, we know. But the crux of the matter really is this:

▶ If you think that POPI applies to how your personal information is being processed by various companies (we promise, it does), lucky you! Because soon your information is going to be better protected, and you're going to have some awesome new statutory rights to protect your privacy.

▶ If you think that POPI applies to your company's processing of personal information (we promise, it does), you need to put down this book and go and pay some lawyers (and maybe some IT nerds) to get you compliant before it becomes fully enforceable. At the time of going to print, we don't know when that will be.

A right to be forgotten?

In May 2014, the Court of Justice of the European Union made a highly controversial ruling effectively granting individuals the right to request search engines to remove links to articles that they no longer wish to be available. The case related to a Spanish man who didn't want a newspaper report detailing his historical debts to be accessible via Google. The court – basing its ruling on the provisions of the European Data Protection Directive, from which POPI draws heavily – ruled that by making the article available in its search results, Google was 'processing' the personal information of the complainant. Furthermore, since the article was no longer relevant, he had the right to request the removal of the link, even if the article was entirely accurate and lawful. According to reports, the ruling has led to thousands of requests from Europeans to have links to unwanted articles removed from their Google search results, including a man convicted of possessing child pornography, someone who tried to kill his family and a convicted cyberstalker.

The judgment raises considerable concerns in that, by allowing people to airbrush over their history, the right to freedom of expression and the rights of the public to access information are unduly infringed. We would hope that if a similar case were to ever be brought before a South African court, greater regard would be given to these conflicting rights.

CHAPTER 9

Keep your fingers out of the digital cookie jar

Intellectual property law in an age where everything is just so darn easy to get your hands on

It is undeniable that the digitisation of movies, images, books and music has allowed for the easy and inexpensive duplication and dissemination of creative works from all over the world. Yet those movies, images, books and music – as well as other digitised content such as videos, corporate logos, multimedia products, software and databases – remain the *intellectual property* of their owners, and are protected by a complex set of national and international intellectual property rights. That matrix of rights is a bit of a labyrinth, and if you have real concerns that your intellectual property is being infringed, or that your conduct is infringing the intellectual property rights of others, you really should get some proper legal advice. But, until then, we're going to help you out with the basics.

Copyright

In simple terms, copyright law aims to protect creative works by providing the owners of those works with a set of rights that only they can exercise. Copyright does not vest in an idea, but rather in the actual manifestation of an idea.

What makes copyright law tricky is that there is no single legal system governing copyright in the world – although there is a degree of divergence between various national copyright laws, each country's laws have their own nuances, and the web of international and various national copyright laws is therefore a difficult one to navigate. That being said, the premise is pretty much the same everywhere: certain works (in particular, films, written works, music and pictures) are protected from being copied, used or disseminated without the permission of the owner.

Of course there are some exceptions to this broad protection. In many jurisdictions, including South Africa, there is a general exception where the reproduction is not in conflict with the normal exploitation of the work and not unreasonably prejudicial to the legitimate interests of the owner of the copyright; as well as specific exceptions for the use of a literary work, musical work or film for purposes of research or private study, criticism or review, or reporting current events. There is also typically an 'educational use' exception, which allows reasonable use of protected works by teachers and educational institutions (for example, during lessons), generally provided that such use is compatible with fair practice and that the source of the work is acknowledged.

In the US, there is a general 'fair use' exception, with the following factors considered in determining whether or not a particular use is fair:

▶ the purpose and character of the use, including whether such use is of a commercial nature or is for non-profit educational purposes;
▶ the nature of the copyrighted work;
▶ the amount and significance of the portion used in relation to the copyrighted work as a whole; and
▶ the effect of the use upon the potential market for, or value of, the copyrighted work.

To © or not to ©

Most jurisdictions do not require registration or the inclusion of a © symbol in order for copyright to vest in a work. It vests immediately upon its creation. Although it doesn't hurt to include it.

Trademarks, unfair competition and passing off

Trademark law protects marks that are capable of distinguishing the goods and services of one entity from those of another, and prevents the use of those marks in a way that is likely to be confusing to consumers or, in the case of a well-known mark, which takes advantage of or is detrimental to the distinctive character or repute of that mark. A trademark could be a logo, symbol, image, design, slogan or word – as long as it acts as a 'badge of origin' by allowing consumers to distinguish the product or service with which it is associated.

For example, in the fast-food industry, the name 'McDonald's' is a registered trademark and protected in terms of trademark law, as is the big yellow *M*, Ronald McDonald, the design of the fries box, and the phrase 'I'm lovin' it'. All these marks serve to distinguish McDonald's from its competitors. All these marks help us identify the origin of the goods – if it has a big yellow *M* on it, or comes in a particular-shaped fries box, we know it comes from McDonald's. Using the phrase 'I'm lovin' it' to advertise your own chain of burgers, or using the big yellow *M* on the packaging of a sex toy, would therefore be prohibited.

As is the case with copyright, the law protecting corporate identity and company marks consists of a complicated matrix of international and national trademark laws, as well as laws relating to unfair competition and passing off. Unlike works protected under copyright, you need to register a trademark in order to be fully protected. Registered marks are identifiable by the ™ or ® symbols.

Personality rights

In certain jurisdictions in the world, rights exist that prohibit the un-authorised use of someone's name or image, particularly for commercial purposes. This 'personality right' is the right to control the commercial use of your own name, image, likeness or identity. This right may act to further bolster claims against those using the name or image of others (particularly celebrities) without authorisation, and prevents, for example, companies using pictures of famous people in their shop window, on their products or on their social media accounts without permission.

Protecting your intellectual property online

Imagine that you're a keen photographer who enjoys sharing your pictures with the world on your Tumblr page. Or imagine you like to blog about cats. Or imagine you're the owner of a successful store called The Lovely Little Cake Shop.

Now imagine that you wake up one morning to find that someone has taken one of your photographs, or your well-crafted paragraph on the mating habits of the British Longhair, and included it on their own website, without permission and without crediting you. Or imagine that a disgruntled customer starts a Facebook page called The *Ugly* Little Cake Shop *of Horrors*, using your store logo as the profile picture.

You'd be furious, wouldn't you?

Well, you'll be happy to know that – unless one of the various complicated exceptions apply – you would in all likelihood have every right to sue for damages on account of infringement of your intellectual property. But the question is whether you want to go through the whole rigmarole of litigation (likely to be trans-jurisdictional – in other words, involving many countries). The answer is likely to be 'No'. We would therefore suggest that you rather:

▶ write a strongly worded letter asserting your rights and requesting that the infringing content be removed *immediately* or you'll *sue*;
▶ report the infringement to the website on which it has occurred, which will then likely swiftly remove it;
▶ complain to your friends over some wine; and
▶ find it in your heart to forgive and forget, and live happily ever after.

Creative Commons

In response to what is considered by some to be an overly restrictive international copyright regime, Creative Commons was established to allow for the legal sharing and adaptation of creative works, in the hope of building a richer 'commons' of information in the digital age. By making various licences available free of charge (everyone loves free stuff!), Creative Commons provides a mechanism to reserve certain rights, while waiving others in order to allow people all over the world to use, build on and share a copyrighted work for the public benefit (think for example of Wikipedia). So if you don't fancy restricting access to your creations, but rather quite like the idea of people being able to develop your ideas and share your work with the world, consider adopting a Creative Commons licence. Find out more about the various licences available at www.CreativeCommons.org.

Your rights in content uploaded onto social media websites

When social media websites go around declaring that, 'You are still the owner of your content!' they're not lying. But they're also really hoping you're not going to read the fine print of their terms of service. If you *did* read the fine print, you would know that, in the majority of cases, by uploading content onto a social media platform – be it photographs, written work or videos – you typically grant the website a very broad licence to use that content. Ordinarily, this licence does not extend to other users of the website, and most websites provide a mechanism through which intellectual property infringements can be reported.

Obviously we cannot cover each and every website, but here's the deal with the big ones (as of May 2014 – for all we know they're going to change tomorrow ...):

▶ **LinkedIn** You grant LinkedIn an irrevocable royalty-free licence to copy, improve, distribute, publish, retain and commercialise any information that you provide to them, including any content, ideas, concepts and/or techniques, without notice or compensation.

▶ **Facebook** By using or accessing its service, you grant Facebook a broad royalty-free licence to use your content on or in connection with Facebook. This licence ends when you delete the content, unless it has been shared with others, and they have not deleted it.

▶ **Twitter** The content submitted, posted or displayed on Twitter is made available subject to a royalty-free licence that allows for Twitter to use, copy, reproduce, modify, publish or distribute that content, which includes the right to make the content available to its partners for distribution or publication, without compensation.

▶ **Instagram** By using Instagram, you grant them a royalty-free licence to use the content that you post, including by making it available to any of its group companies (which includes Facebook).

▶ **YouTube** In uploading content to YouTube, you grant them a royalty-free licence to use, reproduce, distribute and display that content for promoting the service. This licence terminates when you delete the content.

Ultimately, although you retain ownership of content that you upload to social media, accept that the particular website has a wide set of rights in terms of what they can do with that content.

Unauthorised use of your intellectual property by news organisations

One specific instance in which you may find yourself being hounded for use of your intellectual property is if you suddenly turn into a person of interest to a news organisation.

The 'Miracle on the Hudson' – the January 2009 ditching of stricken US Airways Flight 1549 in the Hudson River just off Manhattan Island, and subsequent safe evacuation of all passengers – represents the first high-profile case study of the value of content uploaded by social media users to journalists. Within minutes of the emergency landing, Jānis Krūms had uploaded to Twitter (via TwitPic) a dramatic, now iconic, picture of the downed plane. For the journalist looking to cover this remarkable breaking news event, Jānis Krūms' picture was a must-have. Understandably, the image was picked up by numerous news websites, eventually causing the TwitPic service to crash.

Similarly, when a helicopter crashed in central London in January 2013, journalists were clamouring for eyewitness accounts and pictures. With the immediacy of the link between witness and the world, these high-value news items quickly began showing up on Twitter and YouTube, with witnesses and passers-by posting pictures and videos of the flaming debris long before they were showing up on news desks.

One such witness tweeted (accompanied by a picture):

 Helicopter just hit our building in Vauxhall

In addition to receiving 2507 retweets, the tweet was picked up by news desks around the world. James Laidler tweeted in reply:

 ... James from @BBC Breakfast. Did you take the crash picture and can we use it? We'll credit you

More generally, journalists turned to social media to get information about the incident, with the BBC London Newsroom (@BBCLondonNews) tweeting on the morning of the crash:

 Pictures or video of the #helicopter crash at #Vauxhall X? Send to [email address] or tweet us pls for inclusion in our news bulletin

Although most of us prefer to fly below the radar in our everyday life, there are circumstances when we might just not be able to avoid journalists knocking on your social media door seeking access to your content; because, for the journalist looking to cover a story, social media has come to represent a digital bank of images and content. This is the case not only in scenarios such as those illustrated here – journalists hot on the tail of a breaking-news story – but also in circumstances where journalists are simply seeking out pictures and content uploaded by newsworthy individuals. After all, if someone is arrested for murder, coverage of the story is a whole lot more intriguing if accompanied by a picture of the suspect holding a gun.

Copyright law provides a legal mechanism with which those who want to protect their images, videos and words are able to prevent their use by journalists. Because all original images, texts and videos posted on social media are protected by copyright in the same way as they would be protected offline, a journalist who, without permission, extracts or makes use of an image, text or video on social media and in which copyright subsists, may well be guilty of copyright infringement. Importantly, however, the copying and use of works protected by copyright may be permitted on account of a fair dealing defence for reporting current events, if the source and name of the author (if known) are mentioned. Depending on the jurisdiction, this defence does not necessarily extend to the use of photographs.

> Although dependent on the circumstances, it is unlikely that copyright will vest in a tweet, unless it is sufficiently original. 'Just finished eating my breakfast and on the way to work' is probably not going to be protected ...

The January 2013 judgment of the New York District Court in the case of *Agence France Presse v Morel* was one of the first judicial considerations of the legal implications, in terms of copyright law, of the commercial use of images made available on social media. Following the 2010 earthquake in Haiti, photographer Daniel Morel posted pictures on his Twitter page of the resultant destruction, some of which were subsequently distributed by AFP to Getty Images, and published by *The Washington Post*. The District Court struck down an argument that the pictures became freely available once being posted on Twitter, holding instead that Twitter's terms of service did not give the news agency a licence to publish the images without Morel's permission.

Journalists should therefore take heed that just because content is 'in the public domain' and has been made available on a public platform, it does not necessarily mean that it is no longer protected by copyright and therefore up for grabs to be used in reporting current events. On the other hand, those who find that their social media content has been used by journalists without permission should know that they may have a claim for infringement of copyright. When you happen to be in the right place at the right time, and capture something newsworthy, you might not be so worried about someone using your picture. But if you're thrust into the limelight and news desks are suddenly scraping your social media profiles to find some juicy pictures of you, you might not be all that forgiving.

Tips for protecting your intellectual property online

▶ Asserting an intellectual property infringement is an easy way to get a social media account shut down. If someone is using your corporate identity or copyright-protected work, report the violation to the relevant website. They are typically quite quick in responding to allegations of infringement of intellectual property rights.

▶ Never take to a blog or other social media to discuss an idea. Copyright law does not protect ideas, so if someone steals it before you've had a chance to turn it into reality, you're on your own.

▶ If you run a business, set up accounts across all the major social media platforms, even if you're not going to use them immediately. This prevents others from opening Twitter, Facebook, LinkedIn, Instagram or other social media accounts in the name of your company.

▶ If you come across someone 'cybersquatting' (having registered a domain in the name of your company with the intention of extorting a fee from you to hand it over), get a lawyer.

▶ If you are a professional photographer, watermark your photographs with your name or company logo before uploading albums online.

Avoiding infringing the intellectual property of others

Before the onset of the digital age, if you wanted to copy a book, you had to go down to the library and sit for hours photocopying each page (time consuming, costly and probably illegal). If you wanted to copy your friend's *Now That's What I Call Music Vol. 29* album, you needed some or other special device to burn it onto a second disk (time consuming, costly, and also probably illegal).

Now you can do all of that at the click of a button. Images can be easily copied from the web, films and music can be copied to your hard drive in no time at all, and there are loads of websites where you can find almost anything you want to download – all for *free*!

Win!

Right?

No.

Illegal.

Now, there are hundreds of books and papers written by hundreds of very smart people debating *why* it is that people think it is acceptable to download and copy online content illegally, but frown upon the actual physical theft thereof – maybe it's because we feel a sense of entitlement to cultural productions; maybe it's because the risk of getting caught is so low; maybe the principles of sharing that are so embedded in the Web 2.0 culture have infiltrated our thinking to the point that illegal copying and sharing of digitised content has become an accepted social norm; or maybe we just really, really like free stuff.

There are also hundreds of books and papers written by hundreds of very smart people debating whether or not it is *right* to prevent the sharing of protected digital works and whether it would instead be better if we all just lived in a utopian society where creative industry capitalism is banished and sharing is caring.

We're not going to get into any of that or comment on the rightness or wrongness of stringent protection of copyrighted works in the digital age. Suffice to say that the violation of intellectual property rights of digitised content is happening on an almost industrial scale and – whether you agree with it or not – it is (as of 2014) unlawful.

Of course, it is possible that your use of content falls within one of the exceptions highlighted earlier in this chapter, but it's all quite complicated and tricky to know whether or not that will be the case. So without getting all technical and boring, essentially what you need to know is this:

▶ Just because it is online, doesn't mean it's free for the taking. If you unlawfully *copy* or *use* a picture, text, video, music, software or any of the like from the Internet without a licence to do so, the copyright holders have the right to sue you for damages.
▶ If you *download* copyright-protected content without a licence to do so, the copyright holders have the right to sue you for damages.
▶ If you *distribute* copyright-protected content without a licence to do so (for example, by uploading it online, making it available on a peer-to-peer sharing website or distributing amongst a group of friends), you are probably guilty of a crime and could find yourself facing a fine or prison time.
▶ If you use the *corporate identity* of a company in a way that is likely to cause confusion, or in a way that creates an incorrect impression of an association or endorsement, you may find yourself faced with a lawsuit to stop you from doing so, as well as a claim for damages and/or royalties.

But we know what you're thinking: Nah nah-nah nah nah, you can't catch me!

We're sure that's what a man in Cape Town thought when he uploaded the South African film *Four Corners* on peer-to-peer sharing website The Pirate Bay.

He was wrong. In a ground-breaking first, he was convicted on copyright charges in the Bellville Commercial Crimes Court in April 2014, and given a suspended prison sentence. The perpetrator is alleged to have been traced after tweets about the Pirate Bay file were brought to the attention of the South African Federation of Copyright Theft, which then traced him as the originator of the torrent link. Word on the street is that similar arrests are coming.

There have also been numerous arrests and prosecutions on grounds of illegal file sharing worldwide. In the mid-2000s, the Recording Industry Association of America is reported to have sued more than 18 000 people for illegal music sharing. Although most settled out of court, the litigation campaign saw two individuals ordered to pay $675 000 and $222 000 damages respectively for illegally downloading and sharing files on various P2P networks.

That being said – notwithstanding the recent South African prosecution – it appears as though copyright groups worldwide have somewhat abandoned their strategy of individual prosecutions for illegal file sharing, presumably because of a very public backlash. They seem to have now turned their attention to the websites themselves, with notorious file-sharing website *MegaUpload* having already been shut down and a battle raging on to stop the operations of Swedish site *The Pirate Bay*.

Nevertheless, it cannot be denied that the intellectual property industry is clashing head-on with the somewhat socialist attitudes of the Web 2.0 generation, and that it is facing an uphill battle to bring online infringement of intellectual property rights to an end. Until they figure out a way to make everybody happy (a lofty ideal, if ever there was one), we're just going to have to do our best to convince you to respect the rights of others online. Even though we know you're probably going to disregard everything we've just said and carry on watching your illegally downloaded new season of *Game of Thrones*.

Some guiding principles

▶ We understand that you really, really want the new Beyoncé album/new *Star Wars* movie, and that you really, really don't want to pay for it. But please, just go download it on iTunes.

▶ If you *do* happen to (innocently, of course!) stumble across illegal content, never upload it or share it with others.

▶ Particularly if you have a blog, if you would like to use any text, images or videos that you find online, it is always best to ask permission. Even then, you must still identify the source and author of the material. If permission is refused, look for 'stock' content that is made available using a Creative Commons licence or subscribe to a subscription service such as Getty Images.

▶ Although the extent to which corporations can use trademarks to restrict free speech and satire is debatable, be cautious when using protected corporate identities to denigrate a brand.

▶ Beware of creating a false impression of an endorsement or association between yourself/your company and a particular brand or celebrity.

► Be careful of using protected product names when intending to refer to generic products – Frisbee, Jacuzzi, iPod, Coke, Durex, Band-Aid and Jet Ski are all protected marks that are often used to refer to the more general product category.

► Big conglomerates can sometimes assert intellectual property rights to bully the rest of us. If you are threatened and feel particularly strongly that you are in the right, stand your ground and consult a lawyer.

CHAPTER 10

No one likes a bully

Cyberbullying, harassment and harmful communications

go kill yourself
fuck off and die you worthless piece of crap
I will find you ☺
Rape is the last of your worries

These were just some of the revolting tweets sent by Isabella Sorley and John Nimmo to British feminist campaigner Caroline Criado-Perez in 2013. Pleading guilty to sending menacing tweets, their punishment for this tirade of abuse was a 12-week and 8-week prison sentence respectively. Ms Criado-Perez described the ordeal as 'terrifying and scarring'.

Although extreme, what Isabella Sorley, John Nimmo and countless others have demonstrated so abhorrently, is that for all its benefits, the inescapability of a 24/7 connection has seen social media become a tool with which vile humans can bully helpless victims from the comfort of their own homes. From repeated online posts to offensive 'trolling' and violent threats, this sort of online harassment inflicts untold emotional and psychological harm on its victims.

In recognition of this, most countries have some or other law prohibiting online harassment, whether as part of a general harassment offence, or in terms of specially promulgated laws. Yet in South Africa, under the dispensation of the Domestic Violence Act 1998, victims of harassment at the hands of someone with whom they were not in a 'domestic relationship' – marriage, dating, cohabitation or family, for example – were left without an effective remedy.

Cue the Protection from Harassment Act 2011 (PFHA), a welcome piece of legislation that came into effect on 27 April 2013, and provides for the issuing of protection orders against those engaging in harassment, irrespective of their relationship with the victim.

In terms of the Act, *harassment* includes:

- directly or indirectly;
- engaging in conduct;
- that the alleged perpetrator knows or ought to know;
- causes mental, psychological, physical or emotional harm to the complainant or inspires the reasonable belief that such harm may be caused.

Importantly for online harassment and cyberbullying, the definition of harassment includes unreasonably engaging in electronic communication aimed at the complainant, as well as the sending of electronic mail. Harassment via social media and other digital technologies is therefore prohibited in terms of the new Act.

The PFHA's protection order regime is marvellously simple and has already been utilised to great effect in cases of online harassment. In fact, it may be so effective that it can be used as a quicker, easier and more helpful legal tool with which to deal with online defamation (in those instances where defamation and harassment overlap).

It is, however, important to carefully distinguish between merely rude or annoying communications and the criminal harassment contemplated by the PFHA. We think that the Act strikes the correct balance, but in order to ensure that it is not used as a crude and heavy-handed mechanism for curbing offensive, but ultimately harmless, online communications, we hope that in considering matters under the PFHA, the courts remain alert to the complexities of digital and social media communications.

How to get a protection order issued

- **Who can apply?** You can apply yourself, or someone who has a material interest in your wellbeing can, with your consent, apply on your behalf. A child may apply for a protection order, with or without the assistance of a parent or guardian.

- **Where do I go?** You can apply at any magistrate's court in an area where either you or the perpetrator resides or works. Ask the clerk of the court to help you in applying for a protection order in terms of the Regulations to the PFHA. You do not need legal assistance, although an attorney will be able to help.

- **What then?** The clerk of the court will give you an information notice and explain the process to be followed. Complete an application in the form of an affidavit as prescribed by the Regulations to the PFHA. This will require you to fill out all the details of the alleged harassment. Beware, however, that it is a criminal offence to make a false statement in this affidavit.

- **What if I don't want the whole world to know about it?** The court may order that proceedings be held behind closed doors and that the identity of the relevant persons not be disclosed.

- **What if I'm being harassed by an anonymous person?** If the identity of the perpetrator of electronic harassment is not known, the court may direct the relevant service provider to hand over to the court all identifying information about the perpetrator. The court may also order a police investigation into the name and address of the person harassing you.

▶ **When is a protection order issued?** If the court is convinced that it is warranted, it will issue an *interim* (temporary) protection order against the alleged perpetrator. A copy of the interim protection order will be served on the alleged perpetrator, who will then be required to come to court on a specific date in order to show why the interim order should not be made final.

▶ **What happens on the return date?** On the return date, the court will hear the matter properly and may then decide to issue a *permanent* protection order, prohibiting the perpetrator from engaging in harassment and outlining any other necessary restrictions.

▶ **How long is a permanent protection order valid for?** A final protection order is valid for at least five years.

▶ **What happens if my harasser breaches the order?** If the perpetrator fails to comply with either an interim or permanent protection order, he or she will face a fine or up to five years in prison.

▶ **Does a protection order stop me from laying criminal charges?** No. You are allowed to lodge a criminal complaint against the perpetrator in addition to applying for a protection order.

CHAPTER 11

Don't be a racist. Ever. But in particular, don't be a racist online

The prohibition of hate speech

 Just, well took on an arrogant and disrespectful k***** inside Spar. Should have punched him, should have

– Winner of FHM Modelbook 2011, Twitter (May 2012)

 Dear Mr Peter Mokaba. I wish all whites had been killed when you sang "Kill the Boer", then we wouldn't have to experience [the above] racism

– Twitter user, in response to the model's tweet, Twitter (May 2012)

So erupted one of South Africa's first firestorms regarding hate speech on social media. The tweets elicited numerous complaints to the South African Human Rights Commission and, after a public outcry, the young woman at the heart of the scandal was stripped of her *FHM* title and sponsorship. The whole saga was finally resolved when both women apologised after sharing a very public kumbaya moment.

A similar firestorm faced a young journalist, following this Facebook post in January 2013:

 On 27 March 2013, I will send out an invite to invite you to come to the Westdene Dam for a BIG Black Braai, (100% Blacks), fireworks, DJ – Black-People, celebrating their death … we will always celebrate the death of whiteness

The comments related to the Westdene Dam disaster of 1985, in which 42 white children were killed when their school bus plunged into a dam in Johannesburg. He also posted the names of 24 of the children who had lost their life, commenting that their deaths were 'much appreciated, my Lord!' No fewer than 13 complaints were made to the South African Human Rights Commission, culminating in a mediation session between the Facebook user and some of the complainants. Expressing both remorse and regret, he made an unequivocal apology to the families of the victims, as well as the general South African public. In terms of a settlement agreement, he undertook to, amongst other things, clean the graves of the victims and place flowers at their tombstones.

Sadly, these hateful words and actions are not a new phenomenon, but as we've discussed, social media does have a tendency to bring out the very ugliest side of people. The social media posts highlighted here are just some of the horribly fitting examples of that, and the South African Human Rights Commission has expressed its concern about the growing number of instances in which people have used social media to articulate hurtful and offensive messages.

But the problem of hateful content being posted on social media is not restricted to South Africa. In 2014, a young Muslim couple was jailed in the UK after posting three highly offensive videos on YouTube glorifying the murder of British soldier Lee Rigby, talking about how British troops would be killed on London's streets, and laughing as they drove past flowers laid at the scene of the murder. Facebook also regularly sees hateful pages pop up, such as 'Jewish Ritual Murder' and 'Violently Raping Your Friend Just For Laughs'.

So what is hate speech? Hate speech, which is prohibited in terms of the Promotion of Equality and Prevention of Unfair Discrimination Act 2000 (PEPUDA), is:

▶ words;
▶ based on one or more of the 'prohibited grounds' – race, gender, marital status, ethnic or social origin, colour, sexual orientation, religion and other matters impacting human dignity and equality;
▶ against any person;
▶ that could reasonably be construed to demonstrate a clear intention to be hurtful, be harmful or incite harm, or promote or propagate hatred.

Can we really prohibit speech that is *hurtful*? We think that that goes a bit far, and does not properly strike the balance between dignity, equality and free speech. But that's something for another book!

If something you say online does amount to hate speech, you'll probably find yourself sitting sheepishly before the South African Human Rights Commission, which has a constitutionally mandated duty to monitor and assess the observance of human rights in South Africa. Luckily for you, hate speech is not a crime (yet!), and the Human Rights Commission is not that into punishing people. Rather, you're likely to have to gather around, talk about your feelings, apologise and undertake a bit of restorative justice.

Your content may also fall foul of the content policy of the particular social media platform to which you posted it. Facebook, for example, will remove content that amounts to a direct and serious attack on any protected category of people, although this does not include content that is merely distasteful, offensive or controversial. Similarly, YouTube does not permit content that attacks or demeans a group based on race or ethnic origin, religion, disability, gender, age, veteran status, and sexual orientation or gender identity.

But remember, most social media websites are based in America, and the Americans are pretty serious about freedom of expression. One of the most notorious examples of this was the furore surrounding the film *The Innocence of Muslims*, which was uploaded onto YouTube in July 2012. Perceived as denigrating the prophet Muhammad, the video led to violent protests in many Arab and Muslim nations. Although YouTube has now voluntarily blocked the video in certain countries, Google (remember, they own YouTube) has said that the video does not violate its prohibition on hate speech. Recently, however, the United States Court of Appeals ordered YouTube to remove the video. Why? Not because it amounted to hate speech, but rather on account of one of the actresses objecting to its content on copyright grounds.

So maybe you're reading this thinking that hate speech on social media is not such a big deal, after all. We're not even going to start on the fact that you shouldn't even be *thinking* things that propagate hatred and incite violence, but at the end of the day, you're just going to get a slap on the wrist from the Human Rights Commission, and the big scary American companies are probably not going to do anything to stop you.

So what's all the fuss about?

Your reputation. Remember how we told you how the *reputational* consequences of getting it wrong on social media are often so much more serious than the legal consequences? What do you think the first thing is that pops up when you google the name of any of the people we've discussed in this chapter? We'll give you a hint: it's not anything relating to the good that they do or their successes in life. It is, instead, endless articles reminding the world of their disgraceful comments.

The Internet doesn't forget. The 'racist' label is likely to haunt them for many years to come.

So if you *do* wake up one day feeling particularly hateful and gross, please just take a breath, think about cuddly bunnies, and choose to fill your brain with kind and decent thoughts instead. Because if you do go ahead and rant on social media, we guarantee that you're going to get fired or expelled from school, and for the rest of your life everyone in the whole world will know you as 'That Hate Speech Idiot With No Friends and No Job'.

Don't joke about bombs (LOL!)

Threatening and menacing communications

Remember the tale of poor Paul Chambers, who flippantly tweeted about blowing up Robin Hood Airport, and spent the next three years of his life (and a lot of money) trying to explain the joke to some very serious judges?

Well, unfortunately, Paul Chambers was just the first in a long line of people getting into trouble for what they thought was a joke, but what have rather been deemed – by the authorities, at least – to be menacing or threatening communications. It seems that people throughout the world haven't quite cottoned on to the fact that joking about bombs, murder or rape isn't very funny.

▶ **Australia** In 2013, a 16-year-old boy was dragged from a crowd of 12 000 fans at a Pink concert in Melbourne and arrested after tweeting:

> @Pink I'm ready with my Bomb. Time to blow up #RodLaverArena. B*tch

The tweet was allegedly in reference to a Pink song called 'Timebomb'. The security services monitoring mentions of #RodLaverArena on social media apparently didn't get the reference.

▶ **USA** Upon landing at Los Angeles International Airport in 2012, two British students were interrogated by US law enforcement, barred from entering the US and sent straight back on the first plane home. Why?

Well, it turns out that Homeland Security agents had been monitoring their Twitter feeds, which included:

> 3 weeks today, we're totally in LA pissing people off on Hollywood Blvd and diggin' Marilyn Monroe up!

free for a quick gossip/prep this week before I go destroy America? x

Their ordeal included being thrown into jail overnight with drug smugglers and having their luggage searched for spades. What Homeland Security didn't know was that in the UK 'destroy' also means 'party', and that their luggage was probably just filled with tequila.

▶ **Netherlands** When 14-year-old Twitter user Sarah tweeted at the official account of American Airlines in 2014, she probably thought she was being hilarious:

 hello my name's Ibrahim and I'm from Afghanistan. I'm part of Al Qaida and on June 1st I'm gonna do something really big bye

But when American Airlines responded:

 Sarah, we take these threats very seriously. Your IP address and details will be forwarded to security and the FBI

She probably wished she'd kept her hilarity to herself.
    In the numerous apologetic tweets to American Airlines that followed, she wrote things like:

 pls I'm so scared ... I'm not a terrorist pls

and:

 I was joking and it was my friend not me. Take her IP address not mine

Noting her new-found infamy, she also tweeted that she always wanted to be famous:

 but I meant like Demi Lovato famous, not Osama bin laden famous

Following an independent investigation launched by Dutch law enforcement, Sarah turned herself in. She was brought before a court and subsequently released. She will, presumably, never make a joke ever again.
    Interestingly, in a case of Twitter users rallying around their own,

numerous bomb threats were teasingly sent to American Airlines in the days that followed the young girl's plight going viral. As far as we are aware, none resulted in arrest.

▶ **USA** In the wake of the 2012 Sandy Hook school shooting, a young boy posted a rambling Facebook status including comments such as:

 Kids were shot. Who cares? Dead kids are dead kids. Murder is a good thing ... This is a serious status ... I have been saying for years now that there needs to be another mass murder ... The fact they were kids just makes me laugh. I'd have done this job myself if I could have ... All forms of life are insignificant. Doesnt matter if they die today, tomorrow, or in 30 years. They are going to die. I might as well help them out

Despite it never being viewed as a genuine threat, the 15-year-old was charged with menacing and inducing panic. He was placed on probation and ordered to wear an electronic monitoring unit for 55 days. He was further ordered to participate in family counselling and to complete 70 hours of community service.

Now we should start by saying that, obviously, you shouldn't be making threats. Ever. But if, by virtue of some really morbid sense of humour, you *do* find it funny to make bomb threats or otherwise induce panic, you should know that you're probably going to have a pretty tough time convincing fuddy-duddy police and judges of the joke.

And don't think that these sorts of 'terrorism charges' are restricted to the USA. We South Africans take these things seriously too:

▶ The Protection of Constitutional Democracy Against Terrorist and Related Activities Act 2004 states that it is an offence to threaten any terrorist activity, bombing, hostage-taking or hijacking an aircraft or ship, or to knowingly communicate false information about an explosive or other lethal advice. That means your 'bomb joke' could land you in prison.
▶ Similarly, in terms of the Explosives Act 1956, a bomb hoax could see you imprisoned for between three and 15 years.
▶ It is an offence in terms of the Riotous Assemblies Act 1956 to incite public violence.
▶ In terms of the Films and Publications Act 1996, it is an offence for anyone who is not a member of the press to knowingly broadcast, distribute or exhibit in public a publication – which includes a message or communication made over the Internet – that advocates propaganda for war, incites violence, or advocates hatred based on an identifiable group characteristics and that constitutes incitement to cause harm, and that has not been submitted to and classified by the Films and

Publications Board. If found guilty of this offence, you could be ordered to pay a hefty fine and/or imprisoned for up to five years.

▶ In certain contexts, a threatening communication may constitute hate speech or harassment under the Protection from Harassment Act 2011.

Again, all very legal-y, but remember that due to the exceptions outlined in section 16 of the Constitution, the right to freedom of expression is not going to be of much help to you in these circumstances.

But ... I said 'LOL'!

Although it is arguable that a well-placed 'lol' or 'kidding!' can help correct some ever-present issues with tonality – it is undeniable that 'I'm going to blow up this restaurant lol' is slightly more palatable than 'I'm going to blow up this restaurant' – we advise you not to risk it. Because while the 'I was kidding' defence is the classic go-to of those who get it wrong online, it is often not good enough.

After crashing into a car while driving under the influence (DUI), an 18-year-old woman in Kentucky wrote on Facebook in 2012:

 My dumb ass got a DUI and hit a car LOL

But the people who were in the car that was hit weren't laughing out loud, and reported the post to the court. The woman was ordered to shut down her Facebook page, and spent two days in prison when she failed to do so.

In a more ominous instance of 'lol' failing to quell the masses, a Texan teenager was arrested after getting into a Facebook argument over the video game *League of Legends* and writing:

 Oh yeah, I'm real messed up in the head, I'm going to go shoot up a school full of kids and eat their still-beating hearts

He followed up the comment with 'jk' ('just kidding') and 'lol'. Nevertheless, he was jailed and only released after five months when an anonymous donor paid his $500 000 bail. Yes, that's right – five hundred thousand dollars!

Now may be a good time to remind you about the three problems with social media communications – that they lack context, that they lack tone, and that you lose control over your audience – because they are particularly true in the case of menacing threats. In a post-9/11 world, and a world in which everyone is only just starting to get to grips with social media and some of the histrionics that go with it, law enforcement is probably not going to care that it wasn't a genuine threat or that you were 'OMG joking!'

That being said, as noted by the Lord Chief Justice in Paul Chambers' Twitter joke trial:

Satirical, or iconoclastic, or rude comment, the expression of unpopular or unfashionable opinion about serious or trivial matters, banter or humour, even if distasteful to some or painful to those subjected to it should and no doubt will continue at their customary level.

We hope that we do not see an unreasonable clampdown on such satirical comment and humour purely because it is distasteful to some; but it must nevertheless be remembered that, online, the line between joke and crime is not only a very fine one, but also a very blurry one. So best don't joke about bombs. *Lol* or no *lol*.

Familiarity breeds contempt (and by 'familiarity' we mean Twitter)

The law of contempt of court

If you've never been to court, you should know that:

▶ it's nothing like *Suits, LA Law, Boston Legal, The Practice* and/or *The Good Wife*;
▶ not much furious gavel banging goes on; and
▶ people very rarely shout out things like 'You can't handle the truth!'

(We know. So disappointing, right?)

Court is in fact a very serious place. A place exuding power and demanding respect; a place where people wear Harry Potter robes and bow a lot.

The law of contempt of court recognises the importance of protecting this inherent dignity, repute and authority of courts of law, as well as the importance of ensuring proper administration of justice.

Although contempt of court rules apply to us all, *practically* they have usually really only been of concern to the press and those intimately involved with a court case. The reality of the digital age, however, is that conversations about court proceedings are no longer restricted to chatter outside court, and courtroom reportage is no longer the sole domain of the traditional press. What this means is that the chances of ordinary people clashing with the law of contempt of court are increasing.

Understanding the law of contempt of court

The law of contempt of court is a complicated creature, but here are the important bits as far as social media and digital technology are concerned:

Breaching of court orders

It is an offence of contempt of court to disobey an order of the court, something that happens all too often on social media. The best-known international instance of this came in 2011, when it emerged in the British press that a professional footballer had had an order granted by the High Court of England and Wales to prevent details of his extramarital affair with a well-known television personality being revealed.

When media sources outside of England and Wales reported that the footballer was Ryan Giggs, he was outed *en masse on* Twitter. His name was reportedly tweeted by over 75 000 Twitter users, who in doing so effectively breached the court order.

This led to an absurd situation where the press in England and Wales were prohibited from naming Ryan Giggs as the footballer at the centre of the scandal, despite it being a well-known fact to anyone with access to the Internet. This absurdity was noted by Liberal Democrat MP John Hemming, who told the Commons:

> With about 75 000 people having named Ryan Giggs it is obviously impracticable to imprison them all.

(Wondering why John Hemming was allowed to name Giggs in the Commons? Although controversial, it did not amount to a breach of the court order because of *parliamentary privilege*, which gives legal immunity to members of parliament for statements made in the performance of their legislative duties.)

Despite the cat being well and truly out of the bag, the injunction was not initially lifted. Giggs did eventually agree to the lifting of the anonymity order (hence you get to read about him here, and not some footballer called 'Bob'). Although he did at one point attempt to get Twitter to hand over the details of some of the users who had flouted the court order, the transgressors effectively found safety in numbers.

The same can, however, not be said for 10 people who were prosecuted in the UK for posting the name of a sexual assault victim on Facebook and Twitter, breaching the lifelong anonymity granted to complainants in rape cases. The 19-year-old victim was named (in tweets and retweets) following the conviction and imprisonment of former professional footballer Ched Evans. No fewer than 23 people were arrested, with 10 ultimately prosecuted, despite their protestations that they did not know that what they had done was an offence.

Similarly, at least three men were prosecuted for posting pictures on social media purporting to identify the child killers of two-year-old James Bulger, following a campaign of Internet vigilantism on the 20th anniversary of his murder. The pictures contravened an unprecedented court order that was put in place banning publication of any information on the appearance, whereabouts, movements or new identities of the killers. Jon Venables and Robert Thomson were jailed for life following the brutal murder, but released on parole (with new identities) in 2001.

As the judiciary begins to get to grips with the threat posed by social media, we see more and more judges taking care to specifically highlight that social media users remain bound by orders given by the court. In 2014, a Crown Court judge in the UK specifically warned social media users against jeopardising the trial of an unnamed 15-year-old boy charged with the murder of teacher Ann Maguire, saying:

What's not understood by many is that [the reporting] constraints and prohibitions apply also generally, including online social media sites and bloggers. They are just as much bound by these constraints as are the press. The consequences for individuals, I would emphasise, can be serious if there is a breach.

Although South Africa hasn't yet had any contempt of court prosecutions stemming from court orders being flouted online, our judiciary is beginning to become more mindful of the threat posed by social media. The complexities of the restrictions imposed by court orders extending to Twitter are, however, multifaceted and pose a number of questions that have yet to be fully considered or addressed by the judiciary.

Sub judice

It is an offence to publish anything that prejudices the administration of justice in respect of pending civil or criminal proceedings in a demonstrable and substantial way – a lot of big, fancy words that are essentially meant to stop the media from prejudicing the outcome of a court case.

This does, of course, not restrict your ability to engage in honest and frank debate about the judicial process, and express comments or opinions about matters before the court, but you will run into trouble where it starts impacting on the administration of justice, for example, by influencing the outcome of a case. That being said, it is unlikely that a lone tweet or blog post will ever be sufficient to meet the high hurdle that must be cleared in order for a publication to be truly prejudicial to a pending court case.

Scandalising the court

Unfair or improper criticism of courts, judges or court rulings is prohibited in terms of the law of contempt of court. This does not, however, prohibit you from being forceful in your criticism of the judiciary. As so delightfully noted by the Ontario Court of Appeal in 1987, 'the courts are not fragile flowers that will wither in the hot heat of controversy'.

If, however, your criticism spirals into abuse or false allegations of impropriety, you're crossing the line. The test, as articulated by the Constitutional Court in 2001, is not whether the self-esteem or reputation of judges as individuals is impugned, but rather 'whether the offending conduct, viewed contextually, really was likely to damage the administration of justice'.

Avoiding contempt of court online

The law of contempt of court is a complicated web of statutory restrictions and standing court orders that prohibit the publication of certain information. Although you should by no means feel stifled in the legitimate exercise of your right to speak freely, the best advice we can give you is to

72

be cautious when commenting on, or revealing information about, anything involving court proceedings, the judiciary and the administration of justice, in particular:

▶ Online vigilantism can be very dangerous. Respect the court process and be careful of prejudging proceedings.
▶ Do not identify an alleged perpetrator of a crime before they have appeared before the court and are asked to plead. In particular, do not identify the accused in any indecency or extortion proceedings.
▶ Never disclose the identity of the victim of an alleged sexual offence.
▶ Be wary of naming parties in domestic abuse and maintenance matters.
▶ Do not reveal confidential details of civil proceedings in which you may be involved, for example, an offer of settlement.
▶ Never disclose the names of children involved in court cases, whether as witness, accused, defendant or victim.
▶ It is an offence to identify the parties to divorce proceedings, including any children involved, or to publish any information that might reveal the identity of such persons (indirect identification).

Tweeting the courts

'It seems to me that, subject again to proper safeguards, the advent of court tweeting should be accepted, provided of course that the tweeting does not interfere with the hearing. Why force a journalist or a member of the public to rush out of court in order to telephone or text the contents of his notes written in court, when he can tweet as unobtrusively as he can write? It seems to me, in principle, that tweeting is an excellent way to inform and engage interested members of the public, as well as the legal profession.'
– *Lord Neuberger, Master of the Rolls (2011)*

As we have noted, court reportage was historically the concern of traditional court reporters: those journalists sent to go and sit on the horribly uncomfortable benches in courtrooms across the country, to be the eyes and ears of the public, and emerge with a report of what went down.

The advent of social media means that we don't need to wait for a report to be filed in the lunch break: journalists can now publish what is effectively an almost contemporaneous transcript of court proceedings to the world, primarily through Twitter, being an open, short-form and instantaneous means by which to reach a maximum audience.

Yet the advent of court reporting via Twitter has brought a potential problem to the fore for *non*-journalists. The principle of open justice allows for any man or woman to walk off the street and straight into any courtroom in the country to observe proceedings; it is a fundamental tenet of our democracy, giving credence to the mantra that justice must not only be done, but also be *seen* to be done. This means, however, that any man or woman walking off the street for all intents and purposes becomes a court reporter, without understanding the legal framework within which they are operating and exposing them to a real risk of breaching the sometimes complex reporting restrictions placed on those who report proceedings in the courts.

In South Africa, the default position is that anyone in court is allowed to tweet, blog or otherwise report on the proceedings, and it is standard practice for journalists to do so.

The risks of social media in the courtroom first garnered attention when a complete ban was placed on publication of the graphic testimony of Ina Bonnette during the murder trial of her former husband, Johan Kotzé. The ban extended to any social media reports related to what was testified in court, from both inside the court or elsewhere, until the end of her testimony. The ruling was welcomed by the Department of Justice.

The subsequent Oscar Pistorius murder trial, and associated media captivation, awakened the world to the benefits of tweeting from the courtroom, as the tweets of journalists allowed members of the public to follow court proceedings on a real-time basis. Alive to the potential harm that this could cause, presiding Judge Masipa made sure to extend to Twitter the restrictions placed on live reporting of sensitive evidence.

We fully support allowing journalists and members of the public to use social media to report the goings-on inside courtrooms across South Africa, and firmly believe that it is simply a 21st-century extension of the important principle of open justice. It is, however, incumbent upon the Department of Justice to ensure that ordinary members of the public are made aware of the complex reporting restrictions and rules of contempt of court applicable in any court that they enter, so as to ensure that those reporting the courts do not land up in court themselves. Believe us when we tell you it's no fun when you're the accused. You don't get to wear the wizard robes.

CHAPTER 14

Sssshhh ...

State secrets and the Protection
of State Information Bill*

The authors request that you do not send them angry hate mail and/or allegations of absurdity in respect of some of the legal provisions detailed in this chapter. We know.

Whether you like it or not, there are certain things that the State is allowed to keep secret from the public. And rightly so. For like, safety and stuff.

With this in mind, the highly controversial Protection of State Information Bill aims to, amongst other things, regulate the disclosure of classified state information (currently regulated by the Protection of Information Act 1982). Although initially passed by the National Assembly in 2013, at the time of going to print, the Bill had been sent back to the National Assembly by the president for reconsideration.

As it stands, the Bill prohibits the unlawful and intentional disclosure (which obviously includes disclosure online and on social media) of classified state information. Classified state information is sensitive information about super-secret stuff that is deemed to warrant a big red 'Classified' being stamped on it.

In terms of the Bill, if you're feeling all Jason Bourne-y and *do* disclose classified state information to the public, you could find yourself in prison. Or hiding somewhere in Russia. Currently there is no defence that the information was already in the public domain, although we suspect that that is going to change. Stay tuned!

Some other statutory restrictions on publications
▶ The South African Police Service Act 1995 provides that it is an offence to publish a photograph or sketch of a person who is in custody pending the institution or commencement of criminal proceedings against him or her.
▶ It is an offence in terms of the National Key Points Act 1980 to furnish any information relating to the security measures applicable at or in respect of any National Key Point or in respect of any incident that

occurred at a National Key Point. National Key Points are so super-duper secret that we're not even really allowed to know what they are, but it has been reported that they include the Nkandla homestead; the Union Buildings; OR Tambo, Cape Town and Durban international airports; the Reserve Bank; Eskom's national control centre; Koeberg power station; the Pelindaba nuclear research facility; and a Denel ammunitions factory.

CHAPTER 15

Selfie incrimination

What you post online can and will be held against you

In the decades since its inception, the web has given the world a platform to learn, explore, create and connect beyond our wildest dreams. It is an extraordinary achievement of the human race. Yet sometimes it is also just a place where the extraordinary stupidity of the human race is on show for all of us to point at and laugh.

You see, the culture of oversharing that has been engendered by Web 2.0 extends far beyond people annoying you with every minute detail of their lives and pictures of cats. It has bred a new, extra-special 21st-century kind of criminal: the kind who literally busts himself by gifting evidence of his criminal behaviour to The World. And by 'The World', we obviously mean The Police.

Now one would hope, for the sake of humankind, that this sort of stupidity doesn't happen all too often. Yet there are countless tales of people getting into trouble with the law on account of their social media activity. One of the funniest examples transpired when a Canadian man tweeted in 2013:

 Any dealers in Vaughan wanna make a 20sac chop? Come to Keele/Langstaff Mr. Lube, need a spliff

(For the English speaking amongst you, that is a request for a marijuana dealer to pop by his place of employment to conclude a quick transaction.)

With a tweet that surely sent the man's heart straight into his throat, the regional police replied:

 Awesome! Can we come too?

Luckily, it seems as though the police didn't follow through, and the only consequence of this public quest for a 'spliff' was that the young man lost his job.

Making the police's job just a little easier ...

▶ In Oregon, USA, the police were given a helping hand in finding the person responsible for a hit-and-run in a residential street when an 18-year-old man posted on Facebook:

 Drivin drunk ... classic;) but to whoever's vehicle i hit i am sorry.:P

▶ A 19-year-old woman was arrested in 2012 mere hours after posting a video on YouTube called *Chick Bank Robber*. The video detailed how she had stolen a car and robbed a bank 'with a gun, a pillow case and a note'.
▶ After posting a picture on Facebook showing himself happily siphoning petrol from a police car, a 20-year-old man from Kentucky was arrested. His response? More Facebooking, posting:

 Lol I went to jail over Facebook

▶ In 2011, a man was arrested for burglary in the USA after posting a picture of himself to the Facebook account of the owner of a laptop he had just stolen. In the picture, the burglar can be seen holding cash and wearing a jacket stolen from the same house. Having essentially provided police with his own wanted poster, he was eventually tracked down and arrested.
▶ A man was arrested in Hawaii after uploading a video called *Let's Go Driving, Drinking!* to video-sharing website LiveLeak. The video showed the culprit driving while drinking a beer, telling the camera, 'They didn't say anything about driving and then drinking.' He claimed the video was meant as a parody, and that there was no beer in the bottle.

While the classic fumbling criminal has been a source of laughter for hundreds of years, one can only marvel at what seems like new levels of extreme idiocy in the digital age. Whether it's driven by a search for infamy, a bizarre modern-day need to be the *most* risqué and the *most* controversial kid on the block, a culture of narcissists or just plain stupidity, these stories are certainly good for a few laughs.

Yet stories of people incriminating themselves online are not restricted to comic ineptitude. Many of these incidences are closely linked to horrific crimes, and have helped bring those responsible to justice:

▶ In a widely publicised case in Ohio, USA, pictures and videos of the sexual assault of a drunken 16-year-old girl were key in securing a conviction against the two teenage perpetrators. The matter gained national and international notoriety after evidence of the crime appeared on social media, including an Instagram image showing two boys carrying the unconscious girl by her arms and legs.
▶ An 18-year-old was charged with second-degree murder after losing control of his car, crashing into and killing a 58-year-old cyclist in California, USA. Originally charged with vehicular manslaughter, the charge was upgraded to second-degree murder partly on the basis of his historical Twitter boasts about speedy driving, including:

 Someone come on a death ride with me!!!

 Drive fast live young

▶ In 2011, a 21-year-old Chicago man posted an image on Facebook of his one-year-old daughter with her hands bound in duct tape and a strip covering her mouth. The caption to the photo read, 'This is wut happens wen my baby hits me back'. He was found guilty of a mis-demeanour of domestic battery, sentenced to 18 months of probation and ordered to take parenting classes. He also lost his job.
▶ In 2013, a 31-year-old man from Miami was arrested and charged with first-degree murder after posting on Facebook:

 Im going to prison or death sentence for killing my wife love you guys miss you guys take care Facebook you will see me in the news

He followed this up with a graphic photo of his wife's dead body, with the caption 'RIP'.

What these anecdotes should show is that, from public urination to murder, more and more people are finding out that law enforcement is ever-increasingly turning its eyes to cyberspace. Content that is publicly avail-able online has every right to be used as evidence in any criminal or civil proceedings: whether it's a stupid video of yourself vandalising property, a tweet about drinking and driving, a picture of your speedometer show-ing 240km/h, or evidence of something much worse, it can and will be used against you.

And even if you are smart enough not to post evidence of your illegal behaviour online, you could find that your not-so-smart friend (or a stranger walking past with a smartphone) does so on your behalf. One of the best-known South African examples of this is that of a YouTube video showing two of the notorious 'Waterkloof 4' – jailed after beating a homeless man to death in 2001 – drinking and partying in their prison cell. The emergence of the video shortly after Christoff Becker and Frikkie du Preez were released from prison in 2014 resulted in the men having their parole revoked. They will now only be considered for parole after spending at least a further year in jail.

So here's a new rule:

Never put anything online that you wouldn't want the police to see. And if you do something illegal, make sure it isn't documented online by "someone else".

Wait, scratch that. Here's a New Rule:

Just don't do anything illegal. We've heard jail isn't fun, so best avoid it all together.

PART III

THE COMMON-SENSE BIT

Don't film yourself having sex

This one is so important, we put it in the title

Picture the scene: you finish reading this book and, feeling inspired to exercise a bit of online reputation management, you google your name. Up pops a link to your Facebook page, your Twitter account, and your LinkedIn profile. You feel chuffed, because you've never uploaded any-thing remotely objectionable and look super professional and sober in your profile picture. You self-five yourself for being responsible and awesome. Your parents would be so proud.

But then you see that the next four pages of the Google search results are filled with links to a video of you and your ex-boyfriend having sex, all over porn-sharing sites, with your full name and the name of your employer tagged. You never consented to being filmed, and you are (obviously) mortified. Desperate to not have the matter revealed to the world in public court documents, your only option to escape this nightmare is to change your name.

We wish that this were some horror story that we made up to scare you, but sadly, it's not. This happened. In South Africa.

When private content goes public

Now we should point out that there is nothing illegal about filming yourself having sex, or sending naked pictures of yourself to someone, provided that it is consensual and everyone is of age. In fact, some people encourage it (although you may have gathered from the title of this book that we are not those 'some people'). The problem arises, however, when that sexy video that you made to keep the spark alive suddenly falls into the wrong hands and your intended audience of one turns into an audience of billions. And because digital images and videos can be so easily shared, the chance of this happening is all the more likely.

Here's how:

1. The device on which it was recorded or stored could go AWOL

These things happen. Phones get lost, cameras are stolen, laptops get hacked into, and that private video is suddenly not so private any more.

This was the case in 2008, when the mobile phone of a British university student, containing personal and explicit images with her face clearly visible, was either lost or stolen. The images were subsequently made available for download on a Swedish website, indexed so that the link to the files was at the top of the list of search engine results for searches of her name. In the end, the UK High Court awarded an interim injunction against 'Persons Unknown', preventing all persons from distributing the images.

2. You could be dating or married to an awful human being

If you are filming yourself having sex (stop it immediately!) or sending naked pictures of yourself to someone (ditto!), hopefully it is with or to someone you trust and who respects your privacy. But there are some horrible people out there who think these sorts of things deserve to be shown to their friends. And then their friends think that they deserve to be shown to their friends. And before long ... well, you get the picture.

3. It could go into The Cloud.
Don't ever let it go into The Cloud

We wish we could explain to you what The Cloud is but, honestly, we don't understand it. We think The Cloud is a bit like a unicorn – a mythical Internet server, filled with mythical Internet fairies, where everything you've ever done is stored and where privacy goes to die. In the simplest terms, what The Cloud means is that if a video is taken on your cellphone, it will appear on your tablet and your laptop and every other device connected to your Cloud.

Everything is in The Cloud. The Cloud is terrifying.

4. Revenge porn

We know that you love your boyfriend/girlfriend/husband/wife now. We're sure they're really lovely and that you call each other 'Boo'. But if, for whatever reason, your relationship falls apart (our commiserations), the fact that your ex-boyfriend/girlfriend/husband/wife has access to a video of you having sex, or a picture of you naked, has the potential to turn into your worst nightmare.

This is that scary scenario that we mentioned at the start of the chapter, known as revenge porn. Humiliation at the hands of a spurned lover who posts online, for all the world to see, one of your most intimate moments. There are numerous websites set up for this very purpose, most notably www.texxxan.com (now, thankfully, shut down) and www.myex.com (unfortunately still going strong, operating under the super-classy tagline 'Get Revenge! Naked pics of your Ex').

It is an egregious violation of your privacy and your trust, and there are of course legal remedies available to you:

▶ It no doubt amounts to a violation of your constitutional right to privacy.

▶ It could potentially amount to harassment.
▶ Many websites require payment in order to take the picture or video down – this is extortion.
▶ If you took the picture or video yourself, the online publishing of that picture or video by someone else is a breach of your copyright.

There are also a few countries that have specific laws dealing with revenge porn, including the US states of New Jersey and California, France, the Philippines, the Australian state of Victoria, and Israel, the first country to classify revenge porn as a sex crime.

But really, is that enough? Firstly, even if your rights have been violated, it is often difficult to get pictures or videos taken down because the majority of these websites are based abroad. Secondly, the launching of a legal action against the perpetrator just breathes air into a matter that you desperately want to bury. But most importantly, the reputational harm suffered as a result of a sex video or naked picture being shared online is so damaging that no legal victory will ever truly undo the harm suffered.

So to avoid any of it, just don't film yourself having sex. And don't send naked pictures of yourself to anyone. If you want to spice up your relationship, do it somewhere where technology can't find you, or if you insist, at least make sure that your face and genitals are not visible in the same frame.

And if you think none of this bad stuff is going to happen to you, you should know that when you come crying to us in a year's time about how your life is ruined, we're just going to say, 'We told you so!' Because we did. It's in the title!

CHAPTER 17

A match made in ~~heaven~~ Tinder

Dating in the age of the Internet

So far we've detailed how the digital age has seen people move their every-day communications, social life, business connections and information-gathering online.

But people have also moved their relationships online, with every step in their love life detailed on social media. We tell all our friends as soon as we're 'In a Relationship', typically soliciting hundreds of likes. We post pictures on Instagram of the flowers our boyfriend sent us (#love #roses #spoiled #blessed). We can't wait to post a picture of the two of us, ring on finger, typically accompanied by a 'She said yes!!!!!!!!!!!!!!!!!!!' or a 'I'm marrying my best friend!!!!!!!!!!!!!!!' (because if you don't have more than five exclamation marks, it obviously means you're not really happy). And of course, before the reception has even ended, we post each and every one of the 5 000 pictures taken at our wedding (black and white, of course, and including the obligatory picture of a perfume bottle/cufflinks randomly sitting on the window sill). Some couples have even resorted to including a hashtag in their wedding invitation (#TheJonesWedding #BobAndSueAreGettingHitched) to ensure that social media coverage of their 'special day' is grouped together and easily accessible.

But it's not only the happy side of our relationships that is finding its way online. Un-friending an ex on Facebook is now part and parcel of the break-up process. If you're really bitter, it's accompanied by a snide comment or a picture of you leaping for joy on some or other beach (#freedom #goodriddance #betteroffwithoutyou). And you'd be lying if you said you'd never Facebook-stalked an ex, and taken endless joy from the fact that their new wife/husband/girlfriend/boyfriend is way uglier than you.

The point is, love and relationships play out online, and play an integral role in our online life. It should come as no surprise then that more and more people are turning to the Internet to *find* love. Recent research from the Pew Research Internet Project finds that 11% of American adults – and 38% of those who are currently 'single and looking' for a partner – have used online dating sites or mobile dating apps, with nearly a quarter of online daters having entered into a marriage or long-term relationship with someone they met through a dating site or app. In 2012, *The Huffington Post* estimated that the global online dating industry is worth more than £2 billion. Obviously, the figures for South Africa (which don't exist) would be much lower – perhaps attributable to a low level of Internet penetration, lack of high-speed broadband and increased safety fears – but interest in online dating in South Africa is certainly growing.

So what is online dating? An online (or Internet) dating service is a form of social networking website where users can connect with like-minded individuals with the objective of finding friends, or developing a romantic or sexual relationship. The sites can be quite general, or designed to cater to a particular subset of user (professional, uniformed, married, S&M or vegan, for example). Upon signing up, users are typically required to list certain personal information, including gender, age, location and interests, and are then able to browse the profiles of those who meet their designated criteria. Apps such as Tinder and Grindr provide a similar service, accessible on your smartphone.

All good and well, and in our dreams it will play out exactly like the movie *You've Got Mail*, but there are obvious risks.

Deception and scams

If you've ever been on the singles scene, there's a chance you've experienced the very worst of dating: the creep in the bar who's just a little too touchy; the girl who is clearly after you for your money; the ex who keeps harassing you.

Unfortunately, online, those people have the ability to hide behind a profile that has the potential to be entirely false. The Pew Research Internet Project says that more than *half* of online daters have felt that someone else seriously misrepresented themselves in their profile, while 28% of online daters have been contacted by someone through an online dating site or app in a way that made them feel harassed or uncomfortable.

Being duped is one thing, but online dating services also present a risk of being scammed: having gained their trust with gifts and promises of love, perpetrators manipulate their victims into sending them money or performing favours. And it seems that, while people are quick to scoff at an email from the executor of the estate of a long-lost royal cousin in need of a 'small' down payment in order to send them a very large inheritance, they are inclined to be less suspicious of similar requests from online love interests. In its 2012 Internet Crime Report, the Internet Crime Control Center (a US-based multi-agent task force, with partners including the FBI) reports that it received a staggering 4467 complaints relating to 'romance scams', with victims' losses totalling more than $55 million. More than 85% of these losses were suffered by women, and the majority of complaints came from those in the 60-and-over age range.

Safety risks

There are no doubt thousands of great people online who are upfront, honest and looking for exactly the same thing as you are. Unfortunately, there are also some really dangerous people, looking to exploit the vulnerability of those who are looking for love or companionship. And because online dating usually involves a bit of talking and getting to know each other before actually meeting face to face, the opportunity exists for someone with bad intentions to smooth-talk their way to gaining your trust.

Sadly, there are countless examples of people losing their life at the hands of someone they met online. In 2013, a 67-year-old Australian woman was robbed and murdered in Johannesburg, having come over to meet for the second time with a 28-year-old Nigerian man with whom she had been in a four-year online 'relationship'. That same year, in the USA, an 18-year-old girl was shot, killed and robbed of her iPhone and iPad after meeting up with a man she met using the Tagged app, and a young Australian mother was brutally murdered by a career criminal she met online. And in May 2014, a 25-year-old chemical engineer was found by a passer-by at the bottom of a fire escape in Philadelphia, USA, having been beaten and strangled to death. He had met his killer on Grindr.

To combat these tragedies, a few states in America have passed Internet dating safety legislation, requiring online dating services to tell users upfront whether they do or do not conduct criminal background checks on their members. Whether or not these provisions actually curb crime suffered at the hands of online love interests is doubtful. In any event, we do not have any such legislation in South Africa.

- ► If you do decide to meet someone face to face, tell a friend or family member where you are meeting, and give them as much information as possible about your date.
- ► Try to do as much (lawful!) digging on a date before you meet up – not very romantic, but that is what social media is there for!
- ► When meeting up with someone, do so in a public place and never agree to them picking you up or dropping you off at home.
- ► On dates, do not leave your drink or personal possessions unattended.

Privacy

The personal information that you provide to online dating websites is valuable, particularly where the service is provided for 'free' – you are essentially paying for it with your personal data, and have no right to expect that that data is not going to be exploited.

If you actually took the time to read the terms and conditions of the dating website you sign up to, you'd be in for a shock: many provide that the website has the right to share the content of dating profiles, including photographs, with advertisers, and to use that content in promotional material and on the websites of media partners. Users furthermore grant the website owners an extensive licence to use, copy and distribute the information, content and photographs posted by users on the site. In using these websites, you may even be assigning all copyright in your profile and photographs to the website, and waiving all rights to be identified as the owner of the photograph, in any jurisdiction in the world.

The crux: by signing up to most online dating services, you essentially lose control over the information and pictures that you provide to them. It is up to you to decide whether or not this is something that you are willing to accept in exchange for the service.

In addition to privacy concerns raised by their use of the personal information, Internet dating services also pose a risk of identity theft. Although this is a phenomenon that is by no means restricted to online dating – the risk of identity theft exists on any online service or social media website to which you provide personal information and photographs (see Chapter 19) – there may be a heightened risk of identity theft on online dating websites.

Offering up your information

- ► Read the terms and conditions and privacy policy of any online dating service that you sign up for.
- ► Make your username as generic as possible and avoid including things like your year of birth or surname.
- ► Never include your personal information – full name, ID number, email address, telephone number, employer or

other identifying information – in your online dating profile.
- ▶ Immediately stop talking to anyone who pressures you for personal or financial information.
- ▶ If you do eventually start talking via email, consider initially setting up a separate email address for the purpose that does not include your surname.

We hope that all this doesn't put you off online dating, because in the digital age more and more people will look to the Internet for love, and there is every chance that that search will be successful.

So please, sign up. With our blessing. And when it all works out, you can send us your wedding pictures, and we promise to gush over them (although be warned that we *will* judge you if you adopt a hashtag for your wedding or take a photo of your perfume bottle). But please just be vigilant. There are, unfortunately, some horrible people out there.

CHAPTER 18

What do you do with a drunken tweeter?

Don't tweet when you're drunk

We're gonna let you in on a little secret, if you promise that you won't hold us to it, and that you definitely won't go out testing the theory: if you're going to be committing a crime, sometimes it kinda helps to be really, really drunk. You see, the commission of a crime requires you to have criminal capacity – something that you may not have if you're so hopelessly drunk that you have no clue what you're doing.

In 2012, British student Liam Stacey discovered that this doesn't necessarily apply on social media. One Saturday in March, Liam had been drinking since lunchtime. Utterly inebriated, he watched as Tottenham Hotspurs footballer Fabrice Muamba collapsed on the pitch during an FA Cup tie, having suffered a cardiac arrest. Stupidly, Liam decided to hop on Twitter and post something vile and racist about Muamba, as well as tweet offensive responses to those who dared to challenge his behaviour.

He was arrested at his student house, and sentenced to 56 days in prison. He was also suspended from university and de-registered as a player with his rugby club.

If Liam Stacey can teach you anything, let it be that you should never, ever do or say anything on social media when you're drunk. We know that once you've had a few beers, you think you're the funniest, smartest person in the whole wide world, and also that you're a pretty awesome dancer. But you're not. And that drunken dalliance with social media will only serve to reveal to the world exactly how unfunny and embarrassing you are. Come to think of it, perhaps that's punishment enough.

CHAPTER 19

Stop making criminals' lives easier

Keeping yourself safe in the digital age

Remember how, at the very beginning, we spoke about how social media has bred a culture of oversharing information? And how that is a cause for concern? Well, you know who doesn't think that it is a cause for concern? *Criminals*.

Criminals think it's awesome.

We are a nation that fiercely guards our safety and security. We live behind high walls, armed with fancy alarm systems and burglar bars, and are suspicious of people knocking on our door.

Yet every single day, hundreds of thousands of people flout their natural instincts to guard their safety and security by *gifting* criminals the sort of information that – in the real world – they would never choose to share.

▶ 'Just signed the offer to purchase our new house! Yippee! #homeowner' (posted together with a picture of an offer document with full name, address and signature)
▶ 'Finally I got my new passport!!!!!' (posted together with a picture showing full name, picture, date of birth and passport number)
▶ 'Hubby working late. Home alone. Boo:('
▶ 'Going away for three weeks of blissful holiday! See you later Joburg!'

At the time, it all feels pretty innocuous, but every time you post this sort of information online, a criminal somewhere rubs his hands together deliriously and laughs like an evil genius.

**If you go down to the woods today ...
you better not geotag your photos**

The online sharing of your bush-break photos is leading poachers directly to rhino and other endangered species. So make sure you do not have the geotag function enabled and never disclose where your pictures were taken.

Think of the dangers

Don't, however, think that just being a little more cautious about what you post online is going to be enough to keep you safe. There will always be bad people trying to hurt and take advantage of good people – unfortunately, the digitisation of information and the ease of connection made possible by the Internet just makes it that much easier for them to do so.

Identity theft and malicious impersonation

As technology gets more and more sophisticated, and we become more accustomed to sharing data online, it becomes easier for criminals to go about their job of being terrible humans. Disclosing private information online (however innocuous), as well as hacking, viruses and spyware, all allow criminals to infiltrate your data. This information could be used to, amongst other things:

▶ commit identity theft;
▶ commit numerous financial frauds; or
▶ set up false online profiles in your name, in order to bully or harass you or tarnish your reputation.

But even if you're not explicitly posting personal information online, details about your identity can be *inferred* from your conduct. For example, a recent US study of 58 000 Facebook users was able to accurately determine the race, IQ, sexuality, substance use, personality and political views of users just by analysing their 'likes'.

Online exposure to real-world criminals

By detailing your banal comings and goings online, you effectively gift criminals CCTV footage of your life. Not only does this expose you to obvious physical harm (for example, by a criminal accosting you in your home or workplace), but it also makes it easier for strangers to gain your trust by purporting to know intimate details of your life.

One of the most tragic cases of betrayal by an online contact came in 2004, and saw pregnant Bobbie Jo Stinnett lose her life. Bobbie Jo had arranged to meet up with the prospective buyer of a terrier, whom she had met in an online chatroom, at her home in Missouri, USA. She was later found murdered with her premature baby cut from her womb. Her killer, Lisa M Montgomery, was sentenced to death. Bobbie Jo's baby daughter survived and was reunited with her father.

In 2013, 53-year-old Richard Beasley was sentenced to death in Ohio for the murder of three men who had responded to an advertisement for a job posted by Beasley on popular classifieds website Craigslist. Similarly, in Massachusetts, Philip Markoff was indicted on charges of first-degree murder and armed robbery in relation to attacks on three women who had posted personal advertisements on Craigslist. In 2010, while awaiting trial, Markoff killed himself in his prison cell.

Phishing and scams

From the classic 419 Scam to unsolicited requests for personal information, we've all heard some or other story of a vulnerable victim losing their life savings to an online scam. Although it is perhaps easy to deride a 'fool' who so easily fell for an 'obvious' fraud, confidence tricksters have now well and truly moved into the 21st century, and you'd be foolish to think that you are incapable of falling victim to increasingly smart online crooks.

Guarding your online (and offline) safety

'If you tell me your date of birth and where you're born [on Facebook] I'm 98% [of the way] to stealing your identity ... Never state your date of birth and where you were born [on personal profiles], otherwise you are saying "come and steal my identity".'
– *Frank Abagnale, security consultant and former conman, portrayed by Leonardo DiCaprio in the film Catch Me If You Can*

Step 1: Put up proper technological defences

▶ Install effective antivirus software and make sure to keep it updated.
▶ Ensure you have strong, unique passwords for all your online accounts. As hard as it is to remember hundreds of different passwords, avoid having the same one across all your online accounts. At the very least, your online banking password should be unique.
▶ Only use secure Wi-Fi networks.
▶ Utilise the settings available to make your social media profiles as private as possible (this includes Instagram and Facebook photo albums). We appreciate that a closed Twitter profile, YouTube account or blog defeats the whole point, so just be extra cautious about what you post on these platforms, and understand that the whole world will have access to it.

Step 2: Guard your personal and financial information

▶ Never share your account login details with *anyone*.
▶ Your social media profile should contain as little personal information as possible. Remove any references to your address and telephone number, and do not include your year of birth. Some experts also warn

against sharing your hometown, relationship status, school location and graduation dates.

▶ Think about the answers to your security questions (pet names, mother's maiden name or child's name, for example) and make sure you're not putting that information online.

▶ On closed networks, carefully consider who you allow to join your circle of contacts. Delete everyone you do not know from your friends list. Do not accept friend requests from strangers.

▶ Never hand over your bank details, credit card information, money or personal information in response to unsolicited emails.

▶ As much as possible, arrange for paperless bills and financial statements.

Step 3: Be security conscious

▶ Do not use any website unless you are completely comfortable with its security and privacy features.

▶ If you do conduct any online business – purchases, sales or interactions with online service providers – do research into the legitimacy of the website that you are using. If dealing with a private individual, ask as many questions as you need to reassure yourself. Make contact with them before transferring any money. Be extra cautious about going to their home, or allowing them into yours, in order to finalise the transaction.

▶ If you receive a communication telling you that you've won a prize in a competition you didn't enter, it's a scam. Back away slowly.

▶ Be conscious of cloning. If someone is already part of your network, do not accept a second 'friend request'. This is likely to be a cloned account, looking to gain access to your information.

▶ Don't click on links or open attachments unless you trust the source.

▶ Do not open spam. Delete it immediately.

▶ Make sure you keep track of your credit card statements so that you can spot any unauthorised charges.

▶ Always log out of your online accounts properly.

Step 4: Think before you post

▶ Before posting anything online, take a second to think about how it could be used to your detriment should it fall into the wrong hands.

▶ Avoid posting pictures of your home, workplace or school, or anything that could reveal private information about yourself.

▶ Never choose a passport-style photograph as a profile picture.

▶ Never 'check-in' at home. People don't need to know where you live.

▶ Keep an eye out for friends posting personal details about you. Set up your social media accounts so that you approve the publication of any mentions made or photographs tagged of you.

We like to think of all of you – our Readers with a capital R – as friends. We hope that if we bump into you in Woolworths you'll high five us and invite us for tea and cake (minus the tea and with extra cake).

We're also very protective over all of you. We (perhaps naively) like to imagine that each of you is busy reading this book inside a warm and happy cocoon of safety, with pillows made of clouds where no harm will ever come to you – where your identity is safe, where your money is safe and, most importantly, where your life is safe.

And we want to keep it that way. For, like, ever and ever.

So please stop with the TMI*. Be smart and be safe.

*For those of you who aren't cool like us, that means 'too much information'.

CHAPTER 20

Will the real Queen Elizabeth please stand up?

Parody and impersonation accounts

'A society that takes itself too seriously risks bottling up its tensions and treating every example of irreverence as a threat to its existence. Humour is one of the great solvents of democracy. It permits the ambiguities and contradictions of public life to be articulated in non-violent forms. It promotes diversity. It enables a multitude of discontents to be expressed in a myriad of spontaneous ways. It is an elixir of constitutional health.'
– *Justice Albie Sachs,* Laugh It Off Promotions CC v SAB International (Finance) BV t/a SAB Mark International

There is something wonderful about those who are truly plugged in to the ideology of Web 2.0. For them, the ability to not only download content, but to create content, allows for true creativity and engagement with popular culture. For them, cultural icons are there to be appropriated by the masses and fashioned into something new.

It is this trend that has seen the emergence of the phenomenon of social media parody accounts: accounts set up in the name of public (and sometimes private) figures, providing updates in an often tongue-in-cheek, satirical and humorous manner.

Our law recognises this sort of satire and parody as protected forms of speech. And isn't that great? We get to live in a society where we can have a little bit of fun; where we can ridicule the follies of society; where wit and irony are valued as important elements of our constitutional democracy; and where we can use subversive humour as a tool for social commentary. Because life is pretty boring when we take ourselves too seriously.

Some of our favourite Twitter parody accounts
@Queen_UK

Purporting to be Queen Elizabeth II, the account has over one million followers and tweets deliciously boozy updates.

▶ 'Is 2pm too early for a martini? Asking for a friend.'
▶ 'Ok Britain, pens down, bottoms up. It's Gin O'Clock. Time to stop working. #ginoclock #NotYouClegg'
▶ 'Dear those running the London Marathon. Keep it down as you pass the Palace, would you? One has an epic hangover. #LondonMarathon'

(In the spirit of honesty, you should know that we're big fans of Gin o'Clock. And we're even bigger fans of Wine o'Clock.)

@NotZuckerberg

It is unsurprising that the CEO of Facebook is not much of a Twitter user. Step up 'Not Mark Zuckerberg', which pokes fun at both Facebook and rival social networks.

▶ 'Be sure to exercise, eat healthy, and get regular medical check-ups. I want my information about you to be valuable for as long as possible.'
▶ 'If a tree falls in the forest, and no one is around to post about it on Facebook, has it really fallen?'
▶ 'Checking to see if Instagram has any filters that can transform photos of me to make it look like I care about your privacy.'
▶ 'A Google+ account is like a piece of home exercise equipment: you have one, you never use it, and you know nobody else uses theirs, either.'

@itsWillyFerrell

With over 1.7 million followers, 'Not Will Ferrell' is a very sarcastic parody of the comedian Will Ferrell (from films such as *Anchorman* and *Old School*).

▶ 'Gay marriage is legal in 6 states, but having sex with a horse is legal in 23. Good going, America.'
▶ 'Dear Pringles, I'm no longer a child and cannot fit my hand inside your tubes of deliciousness. Sincerely, Everyone over 8.'
▶ 'Some people deserve to have eggs thrown at them … brick shaped eggs … made of bricks.'
▶ 'Prove that lightning isn't wizards fighting. You can't.'
▶ 'Roses are red, Violets are blue, Sunflowers are yellow, I

bet you were expecting something romantic, but no, these are just gardening facts.'

@GSElevator

This hilarious account tweets 'things heard in the Goldman Sachs elevator'. Who knew investment bankers could be funny?

▶ '#1: If you're not dead to someone, you're not living right.'
▶ '#1: Some chick asked me what I would do with 10 million bucks. I told her I'd wonder where the rest of my money went.'
▶ '#1: If I only wanted one drink, I'd go for communion.'
▶ '#1: People love to hate Americans. But if it hadn't been for us, they'd all be Instagramming Bratwurst.'
▶ '#1: The new standard of cool is hanging out with friends and not ever looking at a phone or Blackberry.'
▶ '#1: If I ever 'check-in' somewhere on Facebook, it'll be Mt Everest, Mars, or Kate Upton's bedroom. Not Chili's happy hour.'

Parody and impersonation – and knowing the difference

There is, however, a huge distinction to be drawn between a parody account and an impersonation account – the former is good for a few laughs; the latter has the potential to be exceptionally harmful. We like to think that the queen quite enjoys sitting in Buckingham Palace, drinking her gin, and having a chuckle as she reads through her parody account tweets. But what if you awoke one day to find a social media account set up in your or your child's name, from which inappropriate images were being uploaded? What if you found someone posting objectionable content from a Twitter account set up in the name of your company, ostracising customers and undoing years of brand building? All of a sudden, it's not so funny any more.

What do the platforms say?

Parody accounts are permitted by Twitter, provided that the following requirements are met:

▶ The avatar (that's the profile picture) must not be the exact trademark or logo of the account subject.
▶ The account name should not be the exact name of the account subject, without some or other distinguishing word such as 'not', 'fake' or 'fan'.
▶ The bio (that's the bit where you explain who you are) must include a statement distinguishing the account from the account subject,

such as 'This is a parody', 'This is a fan page', 'Parody Account', 'Role-playing Account' or 'This is not affiliated with ...'.

Impersonation is, however, a violation of the Twitter Rules, and Twitter accounts portraying another person in a confusing or deceptive way may be permanently suspended. Our own Chief Justice, Mogoeng Mogoeng, had a run-in with a Twitter impersonation account in his name, which was ultimately shut down. Julius Malema took a different approach – after the ANC Youth League called for the 'closer of Twitter' if its administrators did not respond to reports of various impersonators of Malema, he eventually took over the @Julius_S_Malema account from its originator, followers and all!

Facebook's Statement of Rights and Responsibilities prohibits the creation of an account for anyone other than yourself. If someone is pretending to be you on Facebook, a mechanism exists for this to be reported. Similarly, Instagram allows you to report an impersonation account, and YouTube will remove an account that was established to impersonate another channel or individual.

The law can protect you against malicious impersonation

Irrespective of the fact that most websites prohibit impersonation accounts, as is so often the case, it is not guaranteed that you will have any success in getting such an account removed by the relevant platform. But all hope is not lost, because there may be other laws at your disposal. An impersonation account may, for example, amount to:

▶ *Trademark infringement or infringement of a right of publicity*
This was the case where a Twitter account was set up in the name of the actor James Dean. Obviously the @JamesDean tweets were not from Dean himself – he was killed in a car accident long before the advent of social media – but the account bio did not distinguish the account as being a fan or parody account.

Because there was no chance of confusing the tweets of the @JamesDean account with that of the long-deceased James Dean, Twitter did not suspend the account. So the company that controls the actor's commercial estate responded by filing a complaint on the grounds of, amongst other things, trademark infringement, false endorsement and infringement of Dean's right of publicity (a right to commercial use of your own image). Twitter has since suspended the @JamesDean account.

Similarly, the owner of a Twitter account in the name of Coventry First, which mocked the life insurance firm by essentially rooting for death, was sued on the basis of unfair competition and trademark infringement.

▶ *Harassment*
The state of Texas, for example, has passed a law in terms of which offenders can be jailed for up to a year for adopting another person's identity on social media to 'harm, defraud, intimidate or threaten'. It is

also possible that communications sent from an impersonation account may amount to harassment in terms of South Africa's Protection from Harassment Act 2011.

▶ *Defamation*
To the extent that an impersonation account damages your reputation in the eyes of third parties, you will have a legal claim against the perpetrator. In the 2008 matter of *Applause Store Productions Limited & Anor v Raphael*, a false Facebook profile for Matthew Firsht was set up, including his date of birth, relationship status, purported sexual preference and religious views, as well as a Facebook group linked to the fake profile, called 'Has Matthew Firsht lied to you?' Having successfully removed the false profile and group from Facebook, Firsht obtained an order against Facebook for disclosure of the registration data of the person who created them. It turned out that it was a former friend of Firsht. In a defamation claim heard by the UK High Court, Firsht was awarded £15 000 in damages, with £5 000 in damages awarded to his company.

▶ *Copyright infringement*
This occurs when, for example, an image protected by copyright is used in the account without the permission of the copyright holder.

▶ *Infringement of privacy*
See Chapter 7.

▶ *Unlawful processing of personal data*
See Chapter 8.

Of course, there are clear free speech concerns in shutting down a social media parody account, as it essentially curtails other people's right to express themselves and amounts to a worrying amount of control over the public meaning of an image. As such, a line needs to be drawn between true parody material and that which is actually illegal, or emotionally, psychologically and economically harmful to people unfortunate enough to be the subject of derisive content.

If you would like to engage in a little bit of fun-poking, by all means go ahead. Just remember that when content crosses the line between parody and malicious impersonation, the law is unlikely to get the joke.

CHAPTER 21

Online voices from the grave

What happens to your data after you're gone

In the digital era, we exist both in the real world and in cyberspace: as more of our life moves online, our social media accounts, email accounts and online banking profiles become digital manifestations of our real-world selves. But what happens to our digital self when our real-world self dies?

The fact is, unless you take steps to shut it down, your digital self carries on living without you, a haunting digital reminder of a life lost.

In many ways, this makes it harder for those left behind to move on. But there are also benefits to keeping a digital legacy alive, affording your friends and family a communal space to mourn. It's really up to family members to decide whether they want your social media presence to carry on without you.

There are companies that allow your social media presence to continue from the grave, by sending a series of secret messages that are published when you die, or tweeting on your behalf once you're gone. Spooky.

But the question of what will happen to your digital presence when you die is not the only thing you need to think about. You also have to think about what will happen to your digital *assets*.

In the days when photos, letters, postbox keys and other mementos were actual tangible assets, if a friend or family member passed away, their life could be boxed up, collected and distributed amongst beneficiaries relatively easily. In the digital era, many of our assets exist in cyberspace – emails, finances, photographs, music, memories – locked in a digital safe, the key to which usually dies along with the owner. This could be potentially devastating to family members left behind, with no way to access a lifetime of memories stored online.

So what happens if you want access to a deceased loved one's social media account? On the one hand, you would hope that it would be relatively easy to get hold of the digital memories left behind. On the other hand, users sign up to these websites on the understanding that their privacy will be protected, and you therefore need to respect the fact that private information cannot simply be handed over. After all, are you sure that you want your grieving family to see every photo you've ever uploaded, every email you've ever sent, and every other aspect of your online life?

It's impossible to deal with all of the social media websites, but the information set out in this chapter should give you an idea about what you would be faced with in the awful event of a loved one passing away.

Facebook and Twitter (The digital diary)

Facebook is tricky, because the Statement of Rights and Responsibilities that binds you as a user prohibits you from sharing your password or letting anyone other than you access your account. This means that it is always a violation of Facebook's policies to log into another person's account – even if they've passed away and they've shared their login details with you.

However, upon request, Facebook will memorialise the account of a deceased person. This does not entitle you to the login information of the person, but rather means that:

▶ No one will be allowed to log into the account.
▶ The account cannot be modified in any way – for example, adding or removing friends, modifying photos or deleting content.
▶ Friends can share memories on the account timeline.
▶ Anyone can send private messages to the account.
▶ Content that was shared prior to the account holder's death remains on their timeline.
▶ The account will not appear in public spaces, so you won't see a birthday reminder, for example.

If you would prefer that the account be deleted in its entirety, Facebook will do so on the request of a verified immediate family member. This will completely remove the account from Facebook, including all associated status updates, photos and other content.

Where a Twitter user has passed away, the executor of the estate or verified immediate family member can request that their account be deactivated. Twitter will not, however, allow anyone other than the user to access the account. Should a Twitter account remain inactive for a prolonged period of time, the account may be permanently removed by Twitter.

Instagram (The digital photo album)

Once contacted, Instagram will remove the account of a deceased person (which will mean that all uploaded pictures are lost). Again, Instagram will not provide the login information to anyone other than the account holder.

Online email accounts (The digital postbox)

Google will provide the authorised representative of a deceased estate access to the content of a user's Gmail account in rare cases only, following a very lengthy process that may include obtaining an order from a US court.

In April 2013, however, Google launched its Inactive Account Manager, through which users can choose to share parts of their account data if they've been inactive for a certain period of time. This will apply to all Google accounts, including Gmail, Blogger, AdSense and YouTube. How it works is that when your account has been inactive for a specific period, a designated trusted contact will be notified via email. This email will contain content that you wrote when you set up your Inactive Account Manager (a bit like a voice from the grave), and contain a list of the data you have chosen to share with them.

A Yahoo account is non-transferable, and any rights to a Yahoo ID and the contents of a Yahoo account are cancelled upon a user's death. Upon receipt of notification of a user's death, Yahoo will cancel the relevant account and permanently delete all content.

Time to start thinking about the future of your digital assets

It's one of the first things you do when you start accumulating assets: draft a will. A slightly morbid experience, but vitally important to ensure that, once you're gone, your estate is dealt with in line with your wishes.

If this chapter teaches you anything, it's that you need to start thinking of your digital assets in the same way you do your house, car and money, because we're pretty sure you don't want your loved ones to have to wrangle for months with some American company trying to get hold of your data.

So here are some tips in dealing with your digital assets:

▶ If you feel particularly strongly about your social media accounts continuing after your death, consider providing guidance to your family in your will as to how you would prefer for this to be handled.
▶ Include a clause in your will giving the executor of your estate, or a family member, the power to access your digital assets and online accounts when you're gone. Bear in mind that this does not necessarily give legitimate authority to these persons to access your accounts, as many websites prohibit users from sharing their password or letting anyone other than the user access the account. But it's a good start.
▶ In order to avoid your executor or family members breaching various website terms by accessing your accounts following your death, you may prefer to include a statement in your will authorising all companies storing your data to disclose it to the executor of your estate. This *may* be enough to allow designated persons to request copies of the data, rather than accessing the accounts directly.
▶ Avoid putting any login details or password information in your will, as this becomes a public document once it is lodged at the Master's Office. Rather, include this information, as well as any passwords to

your smartphone, tablet and computer, in a separate document that is kept securely.
- ▶ Remember that digital music and books purchased, for example using iTunes or Amazon, are treated differently from the digital content that you upload, because – surprise! – you don't own any of it. Typically, when you buy digital music and books, you are in fact simply purchasing a *licence* to use the content, making it very different from a tangible book or CD. Since it's not yours, you can't bequeath it to anyone in your will. The best you can do is hand over your login details and password.

All in all, the days of inheriting a shoebox full of photographs and letters are behind us. It is therefore really worth your while to take some time now to think about your digital self, your digital assets and what is going to happen to your online legacy when you're gone.

CHAPTER 22

We interrupt this programme to bring you some breaking news ...

Newsgathering in the age of social media

When a man in Pakistan nonchalantly tweeted on 1 May 2011:

 Helicopter hovering above Abottabad at 1AM (is a rare event)

followed shortly thereafter by:

 A huge window shaking bang here in Abbttabad Cantt. I hope its not the start of something nasty:-S

he unwittingly – and unbeknownst to many at the time – broke the news of the raid on a compound that housed Osama bin Laden which would ultimately culminate in his death. In the days that followed, Athar tweeted, amongst other things, that 'Reuters got to [him]', he 'spoke to Al Jazeera' and 'last stop, CNN'. He also accused 'the msm' (presumably referencing the mainstream media) of 'milking [him] for news'.

Similarly, the first online record of the Boston Marathon bombings was by a Twitter user, posting on 15 April 2013:

 Uhh explosions in Boston

What followed was a myriad of pictures and tweets from eyewitnesses, as millions of citizen journalists took to cyberspace to report the breaking story.

What these examples illustrate so well is that, in the digital age, the whiff of a newsworthy event is now very often first sniffed on social media: it is the proverbial ear to the ground, the man on the street and the fly on the wall, all rolled into a single digital package. And so, for journalists, social media not only allows them to engage with what the audience is talking about, but also provides a platform from which they can find stories faster, ask questions, crowdsource information, access sources and connect with civilians on the ground who are reporting in real time. Social media also provides a veritable treasure trove of information for the journalist seeking to investigate a story.

Good for journalists; not so good for those of us trying to fly under the news radar. Because while it might be cool to have 15 minutes of Internet fame, when a journalist gets hold of that 2008 photo of you smoking something suspicious and splashes it across the front page of a newspaper, being in the news is no longer so fun.

If you do find that you're the victim of what you consider intrusive newsgathering practices, you're not without remedy, as the same legal and ethical considerations apply to journalists gathering news online as to those hitting the streets to find the story:

▶ **Privacy** Journalists in particular will inevitably come up against accusations of intrusions on privacy. What journalists engaged in newsgathering activities online will ultimately have to ask themselves is whether the particular user has a reasonable expectation of privacy in respect of the content to which the journalist is seeking access. If such an expectation of privacy does exist, it can only be infringed if there is a countervailing legitimate public interest. Journalists should also not engage in subterfuge and hacking in order to seek to retrieve material from social media. For more on this, see Chapter 7.

▶ **Intellectual property** The content collected from social media will very often be protected by intellectual property rights. You may therefore be able to stop its unauthorised use by the media. For more on this, see Chapter 9.

▶ **Confidential sources** Specific rules and laws apply to the protection of confidential sources, and these apply equally to relationships cultivated via social networking. If you dream of being the next Edward Snowden or corporate whistleblower, you are not without protection.

▶ **Over-reliance** Journalists have a duty not to be overly reliant on social media as a newsgathering device and to be wary of falling into traps of defamation and contempt of court. As Barack Obama noted in the aftermath of the digital witch-hunt that followed the Boston Marathon bombings, 'In this age of instant reporting, tweets and blogs, there's a temptation to latch on to any bit of information, sometimes to jump to conclusions.' If you think that a journalist is not investigating or reporting the whole picture, there are mechanisms through which you may question their conduct.

▶ **POPI** The Protection of Personal Information Act 2013 will funda-mentally alter the way information is collected and processed. Although the processing of personal information solely for the purposes of journalistic expression is exempted from the provisions of the Act, journalists have a duty to ensure that their processing of personal information is in fact excluded from the realms of POPI.

▶ **Industry codes** The provisions of the media industry regulations, including the Codes of Conduct of the Broadcasting Complaints Commission of South Africa and the Press Council, also apply to newsgathering and reporting activities on social media. You have the right to lay a complaint against any journalist you believe to be engaging in conduct that violates these industry regulations.

What journalists need to remember is that, while social media is no doubt a new tool in the toolkit of those engaged in newsgathering activities, the key tenets of lawful and ethical newsgathering remain unchanged: gathering reliable, accurate and verifiable news; respecting privacy; recognising intellectual property rights; engaging in honest and transparent practices; and safeguarding the justice system.

What the rest of us need to remember is that we should try not to do anything particularly newsworthy. Or at least make sure that we've culled any embarrassing photos or content from our online profiles so that, when fame and fortune inevitably do come knocking, that old picture of us dancing naked on a bar or stupid tweet about speeding isn't splashed across the front page of a newspaper.

PART IV

THE BUSINESS BIT

CHAPTER 23

From hiring to firing

Employment in the digital age

Time for a reality check: whether you're the CEO of a cool innovative start-up, the director of a very serious and well-established corporate that likes to talk about spreadsheets and forecasts and share prices, or just a plain old employee going about your day, social media has had, and will have, a fundamental impact on your day-to-day operations and that of your company.

It should be ignored at your peril ...

... Okay, yes, we concede that the last bit was a bit ominous and melodramatic. But really – from senior management to junior intern – you need to start thinking about social media and how it impacts on your business. Don't believe us? Then consider this:

▶ If you had a chance, would you not want to check whether your new associate is really as clean-cut as he makes out to be on his CV? Of course you would. Hence, social media is beginning to play an increasing role in the *recruitment process*.

▶ With a voice that can echo around the world, one rogue employee can now tarnish the reputation of even the biggest companies. In fact, one rogue *ex*-employee can now tarnish the reputation of even the biggest companies. Now is the time to start managing your *brand reputation* online.

▶ While we're on the topic of employees, did you know that a joke made on your private Facebook page could get you *fired*?

▶ In an age of oversharing, how sure are you that your *confidential and market-sensitive information* is kept under lock and key? After all, secrets are no longer accidentally revealed around the dinner table; they're revealed online, in front of the whole world.

▶ You take care to adhere to all those important *industry codes and regulations*, right? Those apply equally online, meaning that one employee mistake can get you into serious trouble with your professional regulatory body.

▶ Maybe you knew all these things, and maybe you are open to hopping on the social media bandwagon. But do you really know how to *manage your presence* on these platforms? Do you know about your legal liability for the content published on these platforms? Do you really want to delegate the voice of your entire business to some 20-year-old intern who happens to be the only guy in the office who knows how to use Twitter?

In doing business in the 21st century, those are just some of the things you need to think about. So, are you convinced – you CEOs, you captains of industry, you employees – that you need to take social media, and the risks of getting it wrong on social media, seriously in your business and your careers?

We hope so.

If not, just keep reading.

A paper CV? How very 2002 of you!

Social media and the recruitment process

Gone are the days of your future employment hanging solely on a traditional CV: that carefully prepared document, freshly printed on crisp white paper, in which you try to convince people that you're a leader on the basis of the fact that you were chosen as the captain of the house swimming team in Grade 8.

Alas, the digital age is the age of the digital CV, and more and more companies now consider a 'social media audit' an integral part of their recruitment process.

> Remember Chapter 5. Always consider the potential reputational consequences of what you do and say online. It will stay with you forever and could seriously jeopardise your future career.

If you're a potential employee, we feel really sorry for you. Because these days, that silly picture of you dancing suggestively in a bar, or that stupid joke you shared when you were a teenager could see your job application thrown straight into the bin, without a further look. Your first impression is no longer made with a firm handshake and a good brain, and there is little possibility of a clean slate or a new leaf.

If you're an employer, you're probably thrilled at the thought of getting to weed out potential bad apples before they even step through your door. However, if you are thinking of going beyond using social media as a simple recruitment tool (*ala* LinkedIn), and starting also to adopt it as a screening tool for job applicants, there are a few things you need to be aware of.

Privacy

The same principles of the law of privacy that were discussed in so much detail in Chapter 7 apply equally to the use of information gathered from social media during the recruitment process.

So the question is: does the applicant have a legitimate expectation of privacy over that information? If they have a closed profile, and you're looking to gain access without their consent or by using surreptitious means (for example, using a fake profile to befriend them, or *gasp* hacking into the account), then this will of course amount to a breach of their right to privacy and will land you in some hot water. If, however, you simply want to trawl through their public Twitter profile, feel free. You have every right to do so.

But don't forget POPI. The Protection of Personal Information Act 2013 (discussed in Chapter 8 and, at the time of going to print, awaiting commencement) will significantly restrict the extent to which you can use the personal information of job applicants in screening their social media profiles. Best practice going forward would therefore be to advise potential applicants that the submission of their personal information as part of a job application will entitle you to use that information for screening purposes, including the screening of all publicly accessible social media profiles.

▶ **Job applicants** Utilise the privacy settings available to make your social media accounts as private as possible.

▶ **Employers** Ensure that staff responsible for recruitment have been given comprehensive training and guidelines on the lawful use of personal information gathered from social media. HR staff and hiring managers should also always bear in mind that content found on social media is not necessarily true or verified.

Requesting access

There are reports that numerous companies worldwide, as part of the recruitment process, have resorted to demanding that job candidates disclose their social media account login details for purposes of a social media audit. Cheeky? Yes. Legal? Not necessarily.

In South Africa, handing over account details would technically amount to consenting to the accessing of that account, which will negate any reasonable expectation of privacy that the applicant may have. However, it is questionable whether that consent will be deemed to have been freely and voluntarily given, due to the unequal relationship between company and job applicant.

▶ **Job applicants** If you are asked to disclose your login details, your best bet would be to politely refuse by explaining that:
  ▷ It is a violation of the Terms and Conditions of some social media websites (specifically Facebook) to disclose your login details and password to a third party – bonus points for showing that you're not into breaching contracts!
  ▷ You use social media for strictly personal reasons and take your privacy seriously – bonus points for standing up for yourself!
  ▷ You value the confidentiality of your friends and social media connections, and are conscious that granting access to a potential employer will also reveal personal information about those friends

and connections – bonus points for being a team player and respecting the confidentiality of others!

If the company still insists, ask yourself whether you want to work for a company that has no respect for your privacy ... and then leave.

▶ **Employers** If you ask a job applicant to hand over their login details and they respond with any of the above, give them bonus points for reading this book and hire them immediately!

Discrimination

Unfair discrimination in a working environment is strictly regulated by the Employment Equity Act 1998 (EEA), which places an obligation on employers to take steps to eliminate unfair discrimination in the workplace. The Act prohibits employers from unfairly discriminating, directly or indirectly, against a job applicant in any employment policy or practice on one or more grounds, including race, gender, sex, pregnancy, marital status, family responsibility, ethnic or social origin, colour, sexual orientation, age, disability, religion, HIV status, conscience, belief, political opinion, culture, language and birth.

Unfortunately, social media screening increases the possibility of this sort of discrimination taking place. And, even worse, it is almost impossible to prove; because whereas a requirement to disclose sexual orientation, health or religious views in a job application form raises obvious red flags, accessing that information via social media is all too easy. A Twitter feed quoting numerous Bible verses; an Instagram profile showing an applicant with their same-sex partner; a YouTube account sharing political videos; a Facebook page disclosing a medical condition or pregnancy; or a blog in support of an opposing sports team – all these could be used by an employer to discriminate against a job seeker.

▶ **Job applicants** If you do suspect that you have been discriminated against on the basis of information revealed on any of your social media accounts, you have the right to refer the dispute to the Commission for Conciliation, Mediation and Arbitration (CCMA) for resolution.

▶ **Employers** Don't discriminate, and be conscious of doing so unintentionally. If you're going to conduct a social media audit of candidates, focus on information that reveals illegal behaviour, poor language skills and bad work habits, as opposed to information that falls into a protected category. You may also want to consider outsourcing your recruitment needs to a specialist third-party information gatherer. This will guard against inadvertently coming across personal information that may affect the hiring decision.

CHAPTER 25

Step into my office

The disciplinary consequences of social media slip-ups

So – despite a checkered social media history and a particularly dodgy video of you slugging tequila whilst vociferously declaring your love of big muscles – you got the job. Well done!

... But now, we need to help you keep it.

The first step in doing that is to help you understand that the distinction between your professional and personal life is not all that clear-cut in the digital age. What you do and say online, even if outside of work hours or on a private page, could result in you facing some serious disciplinary consequences, including the loss of your job.

And we think the best way to show that we're not kidding is not to bore you with a long explanation of labour law, but rather to sit you down and tell you some good ol'-fashioned South African stories.

▶ In 2014, a project manager at Ericsson had her contract terminated after she posted a picture of her damaged car on Facebook, accompanied by the following comment:

> Effing k***** taxi. And once again I vote for the death penalty. These savages don't deserve to live. But more importantly [name redacted] is alive and I am alive. They can rot in hell

The post went viral on social media, with the global *@ericsson* Twitter account trending in South Africa. Calls were made for the woman to be fired, and many Twitter users threatened to boycott Ericsson.

Although the employee did issue an apology, a few hours later Ericsson tweeted:

> The subcontractor in question has breached our code of ethics and is no longer working for us

▶ When Justine Sacco, the US-based communications director of a large media company, tweeted just before her flight from London to South Africa in December 2013:

 Going to Africa. Hope I don't get AIDS. Just kidding. I'm white!

she was blissfully unaware of the firestorm that erupted down below. Upon landing at Cape Town International Airport, Justine found out that, while she was busy happily choosing between chicken or beef, her employer had fired her. On Twitter, #HasJustineLandedYet was trending and a spoof account (@LOLJustineSacco) had been set up in her name.

In a funny twist, when the media tried to contact her employer's media relations department for comment, the contact listed on their website was … Justine Sacco.

▶ McIntosh Polela, the spokesperson for the Hawks, was suspended and subsequently fired after taking to Twitter in 2012 to comment on the conviction of Molemo 'JubJub' Maarohanye for the murder of four schoolchildren and attempted murder of two others while drag racing in Soweto:

 JubJub spending 1st nite in prison. Bail has been denied after being found guilty of murder, attempted murder & racing while high … I trust that JubJub's supporters gave him a jar of Vaseline to take to prison

Although arguably protected comment, and therefore entirely lawful, the fact that the spokesperson of the South African Police Service's priority crime unit was making jokes about prison rape was deemed to be misconduct. Interestingly, the offending Twitter account did not mention Polela's employer, but rather simply stated that he was a 'spokesperson'. However, due to the public nature of his role, it is fair to say that the account could be associated with his employer.

▶ In 2013, an *FHM* features editor was suspended and subsequently fired after he posted the following status on his private Facebook page:

 i propose correctional rape and sterilization for any white person who twerks

The same fate faced his colleague, who commented on the status:

 i think rape can be quite fun if executed in a romantic manner. like saying "I love you" before you slip a roofie in her earl grey tea

The men responded by issuing an 'Open Letter to South Africa' in which they apologised for their 'distasteful and insensitive comments', but also took issue with the 'public witch-hunt ... name-calling and demonizing' that was unleashed over the 'private joke' posted on a private Facebook page.

▶ In the immediate aftermath of a woman being killed by the collapse of temporary scaffolding in high winds at a Linkin Park concert in Cape Town in 2012, a South African sports journalist tweeted:

 Linkin Park is so badass, people are dying to see them

The next day, he apologised for the distasteful and insensitive 'joke'. His employer reportedly felt that dismissal would be excessive. He was instead suspended for two weeks and required to attend social media training (not with us ...).

▶ In 2012, a national newspaper published a doctored photograph of the aftermath of a suicide bombing in Afghanistan in which eight South Africans were killed, having digitally removed two dead bodies from the original picture. The next day a photographer employed by the paper took to Twitter with the following:

 ... cloning dead out of pic, unethical unethical unethical!!! Pics ed complained, senior ed staff was ok with it!!! WTF!!!

He was dismissed with immediate effect. His employer argued that he had brought the company name into disrepute by making defamatory comments on Twitter, and that he had further irretrievably damaged the trust relationship between employer and employee. Importantly, they noted:

If you are in an employer, employee relationship, not just on Facebook but blogging, you have to remember to always act in the employer's best interest, that is a common law compulsion.

Don't call your boss a wanker

In 2009, a screenshot of this Facebook exchange went viral:

Anonymous: 'OMG I HATE MY JOB!! My boss is a total pervvy wanker always making me do shit stuff just to piss me off!! WANKER!!'

Her boss (apparently): 'Hi [anonymous], i guess you forgot about adding me on here? Firstly, don't flatter yourself. Secondly, you've worked here 5 months and didn't work out

---

that i'm gay? I know i don't prance around the office like a queen, but it's not exactly a secret. Thirdly, that 'shit stuff' is called your 'job', you know, what i pay you to do. But the fact that you seem able to fuck-up the simplest of tasks might contribute to how you feel about it. And lastly, you also seem to have forgotten that you have 2 weeks left on your 6 month trial period. Don't bother coming in tomorrow. I'll pop your P45 in the post, and you can come in whenever you like to pick up any stuff you've left here. And yes, i'm serious.'

Whether a genuine exchange or just a silly joke, it's a timely reminder to never call your boss a wanker. And to always know just who you've invited into your social media circle of friends.

What the anecdotes highlighted here should all serve to remind us is that the relationship between an employer and employee is one of *trust and confidence*, which imposes a duty on an employee to act in good faith towards his or her employer, a duty that extends to not bringing an employer's name into disrepute and to always acting in an employer's best interests. It is irrelevant whether content is unlawful or not: if you breach that duty of good faith by damaging the reputation of your employer or otherwise, your employer has every right to discipline or even fire you.

The CCMA has been absolutely consistent in upholding employee dismissals on this basis. In a 2011 judgment, the CCMA confirmed the dismissal of both the operations manager and bookkeeper of a company on the basis of derogatory comments made on Facebook about their employer and some of the senior management. The CCMA noted that despite the company and senior management not being mentioned by name in the offending posts, former or current employees of the company would have had no difficulty in identifying the company or persons being referred to. This was sufficient to bring the name of the company into disrepute.

Similarly, the CCMA upheld the dismissal of a radio station employee on the basis of a Facebook post in which he criticised the organisation's board and claimed that its station manager was a criminal.

Advice for employers

Understand that your staff's social media activity has the potential to bring the name of your company into disrepute, and cause serious damage to your brand. It is important to have a social media policy in place to remind employees of the duty of good faith owed to their employer, and that what they do and say online can result in disciplinary consequences.

Dropping the ball

Sports stars, social media, and why sometimes cricketers should just stick to cricket

'Drunk!'
– Chris Gayle, Twitter (15 May 2013)

We, like most South Africans, appreciate sporting prowess. Just like you, we cheer on our rugby/cricket/football/curling stars with fervour. Rightly or wrongly, we put our sporting legends on a pedestal.

But throw social media into the mix and we see more and more of our beloved sporting heroes tumbling off that pedestal, not only getting into trouble with their team and denting their bank balance, but often dragging the name of their country and sponsors down with them.

Now, obviously, the best part about writing on the subject of sportsmen and -women messing up is that the jokes write themselves: off-sides, red card, slam dunk, par for the course, sticky wicket, on the ropes ... we could go on for days. But we recognise that this might get a bit much after a while, so we're going to spare you the cheese and get straight to it.

Of course, despite sometimes appearing superhuman, the laws and rules that apply to sports stars are no different to those that apply to us mere mortals. And just like the rest of us, their social media own goals (sorry, couldn't help it!) can land them in trouble. Yet it does seem as though sportsmen and -women somehow find themselves in trouble a lot more than the average social media user.

Perhaps they only have themselves to blame. Perhaps we should have sympathy for those in the public eye, who are subjected to high degrees of public scrutiny and whose every tweet, post and picture is latched onto by millions of fans. Perhaps it's not fair to throw someone into the limelight without giving them any social media training (we know some people ...). Either way, it seems as though social media + sports star = dangerous mix, as summed up by former Chief Executive of the England and Wales Cricket Board, Hugh Morris:

It is like giving a machine gun to a monkey. It can be fantastic or it can be an absolute disaster too.

But let's not judge. Let's rather gather round and use this as a learning opportunity. So, here's what *not* to do on social media, as explained to you by a bunch of people much richer and more talented than you:

▶ **Don't falsely accuse someone of cheating** In 2011, then Liverpool player Ryan Babel admitted a charge of improper conduct and was fined £10 000 by the Football Association after tweeting, in the aftermath of a defeat to rivals Manchester United, a doctored photograph depicting referee Howard Webb wearing a United shirt.

▶ **Don't be a racist** England defender Rio Ferdinand was fined £45 000 by the Football Association in 2012 after bringing the game into disrepute by tweeting:

 I hear you fella! Choc ice is classic hahahahahahha!!

The comment came in response to a tweet accusing Chelsea player Ashley Cole of being a 'choc ice' – a derogatory term for a black person who acts like a white person.
    Although not fined, Northampton Saints rugby player Brett Sharman found himself in trouble over a racist tweet when he took to social media during the London Olympics in 2012 with a comment directed at British athlete Mo Farrah:

 Good luck Mohammed running for Paki ... I mean Great Britain ...

The irony? Sharman was born in South Africa, but holds a British passport and was reported to have ambitions to represent England. He apologised the next day and deleted his account. Although unclear whether on the basis of his tweet, he was subsequently released from his contract.

▶ **Don't call your employer a '#joke'** In 2014, Blackpool FC footballer Michael Chopra tweeted:

 Fucking joke this come in training only 6 fucking players here then find out the fitness coach taken the football session #joke

He was fined £10 000 by the club.

▶ **Don't wage war on journalists** Following an article in which his form was criticised and his image used alongside a discussion of the dark underbelly of the Indian Premier League, Australian cricketer David Warner responded to a tweet by journalist Malcolm Conn:

 Coming from you champion all you do is talk shit as well. What about encouraging Aus players rather than bagging them

Warner was found guilty of unbecoming behaviour by Cricket Australia and fined AUS$5 750 (about R55 000).

▶ **Don't liken the behaviour of your governing body to slavery, the holocaust or apartheid** In 2011, during the Rugby World Cup and in response to Wales being given seven days to prepare between games, as opposed to Samoa's three, Eliota Fuimaono-Sapolu tweeted:

 OK, it's obvious the IRB are unjust. Wales get 7 days, we get 3. Unfair treatment, like slavery, like the holocaust, like apartheid

The IRB accepted his apology, but he was later suspended for six months when he tweeted that referee Nigel Owens was 'racist' and 'biased'.

▶ **Don't end your career before it's even started** In 2011, a 16-year-old footballer in the UK was fired by his club with immediate effect when he tweeted about how he wished that a parcel bomb sent to Celtic manager Neil Lennon had killed him.

▶ **Don't joke about rape** In December 2013, cricketer Graeme Swann sparked outrage when, in a Facebook conversation with his brother, he compared the English side's Ashes defeat to Australia to being 'ass-raped'.

▶ **Don't be gross** In 2010, Australian swimmer Stephanie Rice tweeted:

 Suck on that faggots!!!

in reaction to Australia beating South Africa in a rugby match in Bloemfontein. She tearfully apologised for the homophobic slur, but was nevertheless axed by her sponsor Jaguar, who also swiftly repossessed her brand new Jaguar XF.

Although his car (presumably) remains untouched, Irish cricket player John Mooney was banned for three matches when he tweeted:

I hope it was slow and painful

in response to the death of Margaret Thatcher.

▶ **Learn from Kevin Pietersen** In 2012, during a test between England and the West Indies, South African-born cricketer Kevin Pietersen tweeted in respect of Sky commentator and former player Nick Knight:

 Can somebody please tell me how Nick Knight has worked his way into the commentary box for the Tests?? Ridiculous

He was fined an undisclosed amount by the English Cricket Board. Pietersen had previously found himself in trouble for his social media activity when he took to Twitter in 2012 to rant about being dropped from the England T20 squad:

 Yep. Done for rest of summer!! Man of the World Cup T20 and dropped from the T20 side too. It's a fuck up!! ...

But why are we talking about cricketers, rugby players and footballers? What does this have to do with the rest of us, those of us whose idea of 'sport' involves sitting at the ninth hole on a golf course, sipping a cocktail?

Well, just as sports stars can get in trouble within their industry – the codes of conduct of the Football Association, the International Rugby Board and Cricket South Africa, for example – so can we get in trouble within ours.

You see, companies and employees are not only regulated by the law, but also by various regulatory bodies and codes specific to their profession. For example, lawyers have the Rules of the Law Society, the press has the Press Code, and doctors have the ethical rules and obligations dictated by the Health Professions Council.

We realise that by now this book is beginning to sound like a stuck record, but remember that each of these professional regulatory codes and policies operates online in exactly the same way as they operate offline.

So before you hop online, think about your professional code of conduct, industry regulations and ethical responsibilities. Take the time to think about how you are often held to a higher standard in your professional life, and how what you say and do online – whether in speaking for and on behalf of your company or not – might see you sitting before some scary board of industry professionals, trying to explain yourself. As if you haven't got enough to worry about. We hope you're taking notes.

In 2013, reports surfaced that 15 gold miners had been sacked in Western Australia after uploading a video on YouTube of them doing the Harlem Shake – a stupid Internet dance craze – underground. One reason for their dismissal and lifetime ban from working on any of the mining company's projects: in taking off their long-sleeved shirts (perhaps to avoid identifying their employer), they had breached the safety regulations of the mine.

Yes, Big Brother is watching.
But so is Big Boss

The privacy of employees

Most cases of employee insubordination and misconduct tend to happen under the nose of the employer: contravening a non-smoking policy, ignoring a reasonable instruction, bad-mouthing a colleague at a communal workstation. If, however, an employee is breaching his or her duty of good faith or damaging the reputation of the company *online*, the chances of an employer actually finding out about it are somewhat slimmer.

Employers would therefore be forgiven for wanting to spend the next few days and weeks tracking down the social media accounts of each of their employees and obsessing over their contents. Nevertheless, what must not be forgotten is that employees retain a right to privacy, and a right to not have their private lives monitored by their boss.

But wait … As the line between professional and personal becomes ever blurrier, is there such a thing as an employee's 'private life' in the digital age?

Monitoring employees on social media

In essence, whether or not an employer is allowed to intercept the social media communications of an employee depends on the platform and whether the employee, in the particular circumstances, would have a reasonable expectation of privacy in respect of the content posted on that particular platform. We've covered this in detail in Chapter 7, but as a reminder, Facebook, for example, allows you to create a closed network of friends by adopting strict privacy settings. An employee's activities on this kind of private platform will likely fall into the 'private life' category. On the other hand, Twitter is an inherently 'open' platform where content is available to the whole world, and employees cannot therefore reasonably take issue with an employer objecting to a tweet posted to the wider public.

This distinction has been considered by the CCMA. In the CCMA cases detailed in Chapter 25, it was held that in accessing the Facebook pages of the respective employees, there had been no violation of the right to privacy by the employer. This was because no privacy settings were invoked to make the Facebook pages private, so their contents were freely accessible to the public. There was, in essence, no reasonable expectation of privacy in the circumstances.

The opposite was true in a case heard before the CCMA in 2011. Having initially accidentally gained access to an employee's private Gmail account while she was on leave, the company's CEO thereafter intentionally accessed the account and came across emails in which she discussed several internal company issues and made derogatory comments about her boss. In questioning the fairness of her dismissal, the (now former) employee argued that the access of her private email account amounted to a violation of her right to privacy, as well as RICA. The CCMA agreed, and held her dismissal to be procedurally and substantively unfair.

Practically, this means that an employer appears to have the right to monitor social media content:

▶ that is generally available to the public (for example, on Twitter, on an open Facebook page, or on a widely accessible blog);
▶ that is made within a private social network to which an employee has invited or accepted his or her employer; or
▶ that was made on a private profile but that has subsequently been revealed to the general public (either by having 'gone viral' or been publicly distributed beyond the initial private account).

You cannot, however, monitor or act on the basis of social media activity to which you gained surreptitious access, for example by hacking, using login information without permission, or befriending an employee using a fake profile. Any dismissal made on the basis of content obtained in such a manner will in all likelihood be unfair.

But I said, 'I tweet in my personal capacity'!

Sorry, disclaimers such as 'I tweet in my personal capacity' or 'Views are not those of my employer' are not going to save you. As long as you can be associated with your employer – whether they are named on your profile or not – your online conduct has the potential to get you in trouble. In fact, sometimes the effect of these disclaimers is to make the association with your employer even more obvious ('I work for X, but I tweet in my personal capacity'). So think of your 'disclaimer' more like an editorial comment that contextualises your posts, rather than something that lets you go wild without any consequences.

But it was outside work hours!

Although we have had no official word on this in South Africa, it is unlikely that the fact that your social media activity was outside of work hours will be enough to save you, as a social media policy can legitimately extend beyond the time you are 'at work' to the extent necessary to protect the business interests of your employer. What goes on outside of work hours is now documented in a digital paper trail; ripe to not only be discussed around the water cooler on Monday morning, but to do serious damage to the repute of your employer when spread beyond the walls of the office.

Monitoring employee emails, instant messages and other electronic communications

To put it simply, RICA provides for a general prohibition on the intentional interception of electronic communications, with an exception in certain circumstances where the communication is intercepted in the course of carrying on business. This is not a textbook, so we're not going to discuss the intricacies of it all, but to summarise, you may intercept electronic communications that take place in the course of carrying on business (an annoyingly vague concept that probably covers anything done on a work-issued device or over an office network), provided that:

▶ the interception is done by or with the consent of the CEO or someone duly authorised by the CEO;
▶ the interception is for purposes of establishing the existence of facts or investigating unauthorised use;
▶ the telecommunication system being monitored is provided for use wholly or partly in connection with the business (for example, the workplace network); and
▶ all reasonable efforts have been taken to inform the person of the possibility of such interception in advance, or their express or implied consent to such interception has been obtained.

> ### Don't forget
> Once POPI commences, the interception of employee communications will amount to the processing of personal information and will need to comply with the eight principles of lawful processing. See Chapter 8.

A company may therefore monitor emails sent and received on its network, provided that prior notice is given to all employees and that none have objected. It is therefore important to prepare a detailed policy on the acceptable use of company resources, highlighting that violation of the policy will justify disciplinary action being taken, and clearly specifying the terms on which the company may monitor and intercept employee communications.

An employer may only monitor an employee-owned device, even during work hours, with the prior written consent of the employee. Of course, that consent needs to be freely given, so no use trying to bully an employee into letting you read his WhatsApp messages ...

CHAPTER 28

Social media in the workplace

Some other things to think about

Whether you have a workforce of two or 20 000, someone somewhere is on social media. This raises a few additional concerns that employers need to constantly keep in the back (or front) of their mind.

Confidential and price-sensitive information

Social media and the concomitant culture of oversharing don't just mean that you have to endure endless pictures of people's lunch. It can also result in very confidential information being unveiled to the whole world.

Naturally, employees come across confidential business information, as well as the personal information of clients and third parties, in the course of their employment. Obviously, all contractual obligations (including those restraining the disclosure of confidential information) will apply online in exactly the same way as they apply in the real world. Yet when a member of staff – be it a 19-year-old intern or a 60-year-old CEO – has become accustomed to sharing intimate details of their life online, the sharing of details of their job doesn't seem all that strange. That same young woman who keeps taking pictures of her lunch, also takes a picture of the piles of work on her desk and complains on Twitter about that transaction that's keeping her at the office. It is very rarely done out of malice, but rather the result of a simple default to over-sharing, without any thought of the consequences.

This was the case when the Chief Financial Officer of listed American retailer Francesca's Holdings Corporation took to various social media platforms to discuss internal company matters. These included:

 Roadshow completed. Sold $275 million of secondary shares. Earned my pay this week

 Dinner w/Board tonite. Used to be fun. Now one must be on guard every second

Board meeting. Good numbers=Happy Board

Once the posts came to the attention of his employer, he was swiftly fired for improperly communicating company information through social media.

Yet the consequences could have been much worse. The CEO of US online entertainment service Netflix found this out in July 2012 when he took to his personal Facebook page, which had over 200 000 subscribers, with the following:

 Congrats to Ted Sarandos, and his amazing content licensing team. Netflix monthly viewing exceeded 1 billion hours for the first time ever in June. When House of Cards and Arrested Development debut, we'll blow these records away. Keep going, Ted, we need even more!

At the time, this information had not been disclosed to the Securities and Exchange Commission (SEC), nor had a press release or post on Netflix's own website or Facebook page been issued. The comment was picked up by news outlets, and between the time the market opened on 3 July and the close of trading the following day, the Netflix stock price had risen by $11.27.

The matter prompted an investigation by the SEC, which ultimately determined not to pursue an enforcement action against Netflix or its CEO.

In South Africa, the disclosure of financial information relating to listed entities is strictly regulated in terms of both the Financial Markets Act 2013 and the JSE Listing Requirements.

The Financial Markets Act states that it is an offence for a director, employee or shareholder of a listed company, or someone who has access to information by virtue of their employment, office or profession, to disclose inside information. *Inside information* is specific or precise information that has not been made public and that is obtained or learned as an insider and, if made public, would be likely to have a material effect on the price or value of any security listed on a regulated market.

The JSE Listing Requirements further regulate how price-sensitive information is made public. Publication of information that has not yet been properly disclosed and that could impact on the price of listed securities may constitute a breach of the law.

> Now might be the time for a staff refresher course on confidentiality obligations and insider trading laws. Remind all employees to think carefully before disclosing any details about the goings-on within the company, on social media or

otherwise, and that even an innocent post like 'Woohoo, we made our budget, we're all getting bonuses' may just land the company in trouble. Information could also be revealed accidentally – when posting pictures, staff should always consider what is in the foreground and background.

Whether or not the Financial Services Board, law enforcement or any other regulatory body would in fact take action against someone potentially having committed an offence by virtue of their social media ramblings remains unclear, and in our view, such action would be excessive. Per the SEC report into the Netflix CEO:

There has been a rapid proliferation of social media channels for corporate communication ... An increasing number of public companies are using social media to communicate with their shareholders and the investing public. We appreciate the value and prevalence of social media channels in contemporary market communications, and the Commission supports companies seeking new ways to communicate and engage with shareholders and the market. This Report is not aimed at inhibiting corporate communication through evolving social media channels.

In a world where the tedium of traditional media is slowly being eradicated in favour of instantaneous access to real-time information, it may be worthwhile for the JSE and Financial Services Board to bring financial reporting into the 21st century.

Vicarious liability

Even where an employee's online conduct does not go so far as to breach the duty of good faith owed to an employer, the employer may still find themselves in trouble.

The well-established principle of vicarious liability essentially means that an employer may be held legally liable for the unlawful acts of its employees, to the extent that they were committed in the course and scope of the employee's duties. On this basis, for example, an employer can be held liable for harassment suffered by an employee at the hands of their superior, even though the employer had not been aware of, or sanctioned, the behaviour. To the extent that this harassment takes place on social media, as opposed to beside the photocopier, the employer could be held equally liable.

The most significant case of this sort came out of the UK in 2012, where Carphone Warehouse was found to be vicariously liable for the harassment of an employee on the grounds of sexual orientation. The complaint arose when two employees of the company used a colleague's smartphone, without permission, to post the following status on his Facebook page:

Finally came out of the closet. I am gay and proud of it

Productivity

The debate rages on as to whether or not social media harms or enhances productivity. Whatever your view, it's really up to each individual company to decide on if – and how – they want to regulate access to social media during working hours or using the company network.

If a company does decide to regulate access, it may involve a simple acceptable use policy, or if they're really serious about it, investing in some enhanced infrastructure to ensure that there is no sneaky Facebooking going on behind closed doors. In any event, if you spot a staffer posting 237 non-work-related tweets in a day, you should rightfully question just how much work is getting done.

Note, however, that none of this will change the fact that most people have access to social media on their smartphone. In the long run, management might just have to accept the fact that social media has become part of the workplace and hold on for the ride.

A digital parting of ways

Termination of the employment relationship

In the boring old days, the termination of an employment relationship typically involved simply packing the contents of your desk into a cardboard box, handing in your access card, and sending a cringeworthy email ('I've loved my time here … thank you to everyone I've ever met … I'm moving on but will never forget you … Good luck to you all … Keep in touch … blah blah blah'). But just as a break-up now involves hopping on Facebook for the dreaded 'Bridget is no longer in a relationship' update, these days parting ways with an employer also throws up a few digital curve balls.

Cutting digital ties

With it becoming standard practice for employees to declare their job status to the world – whether on Facebook, Twitter or LinkedIn – and because we sometimes tend to take things at face value (if Google says so, it must be true, no?), the failure to keep employer references updated can have far-reaching consequences. Simply by associating him- or herself with a company on social media, a former employee can do some serious harm to the brand by virtue of their online activity.

By way of example, when that journalist went on his racist rant about the Westdene Dam disaster on Facebook (see Chapter 11), it was reported that he had claimed on his Facebook profile to be employed by the *Daily Sun* newspaper. The newspaper's publisher was quick to refute this, saying that he had not worked there since the beginning of the previous year. But the damage had already been done. The association had been made.

Media24 (owners of the *Daily Sun*) went on to lay a complaint with the South African Human Rights Commission against the journalist, and was involved in the subsequent mediation. The terms of settlement included an undertaking that the journalist ensure that the public does not have access to any content online that may indicate an employment relationship with Media24.

> As part of standard exit procedure, ensure that all departing employees sign an undertaking that they have removed all references to the company from all their social media profiles (especially Facebook and LinkedIn) that would misleadingly indicate that they are currently associated with the employer in any way.

Ownership of company accounts

In 2013, the social media planner of beleaguered UK entertainment retail company HMV began 'live tweeting' the mass firing of employees from the company's official Twitter account:

> We're tweeting live from inside HR where we're all being fired! Exciting!!

> There are over 60 of us being fired at once! Mass execution of loyal employees who love the brand

> Under usual circumstances, we'd never dare do such a thing as this. However, when the company you dearly love is being ruined … and those hard working individuals, who wanted to make hmv great again, have mostly been fired, there seemed no other choice … Especially since these accounts were set up by an intern (unpaid, technically illegal) two years ago

The incident was picked up by news outlets around the world, and triggered panic amongst HMV executives looking to shut down the feed. As noted by the rogue (soon to be ex-employee) tweeter:

> Just overheard our Marketing Director (he's staying, folks) ask "How do I shut down Twitter?" #hmvXFactorFiring

Also in the UK, in 2013, three former employees were ordered by a High Court to hand over access, management and control of their erstwhile employer's LinkedIn groups, after they refused to do so when they left the company. They had been using the groups to promote their new rival business.

What these incidents show is that outsourcing the running of the social media accounts of a company to staff or third parties, with no clue by senior management on how to operate or access them, can have severe consequences for the business and brand when things go belly-up. By doing so, you are essentially handing over the voice of the company to someone over whom senior management has no control, and making it very difficult to get that voice back.

Retaining control over company accounts

▶ Make sure that those who produce content on behalf of the company are sufficiently trained in the legal considerations of using social media.

▶ Ensure that management knows of all social media accounts in the name of the company and that they have access at all times.

▶ Have detailed policies and guidelines in place governing those who produce content on behalf of the company. If more than one person has access to the account, consider adopting a policy requiring each user to post their initials in each post so that you know who originated the content.

▶ In the digital age, a company's social media presence and followers are a valuable commodity. Set up a policy for those managing the official social media accounts of the company, specifying:
   ▷ that the social media accounts are the property of the company;
   ▷ that any followers, friends and connections are the property of the company;
   ▷ that the login details of the accounts may not be changed without written authorisation; and
   ▷ that the login details of the accounts must be duly handed over and all access to the accounts relinquished upon termination of duties.

▶ If you employ a third party to maintain your social media accounts, make sure that there are proper controls in place to ensure that they get the message right.

▶ If you are 'locked out' of your account by an ex-employee, obtain legal advice. Most social networks do, however, provide for mechanisms to report a rights violation, which is particularly effective if there has been an intellectual property rights infringement.

Ownership of employee accounts

In certain lines of business, employees find it particularly valuable to engage directly with consumers, build recognition and develop business connections through their own social media accounts (most notably,

LinkedIn and Twitter). This is different from an official company account – this is Joe Blogs setting up his own account and using it in the course and scope of his employment in order to create business for his employer.

So what happens when Joe Blogs leaves Company X and goes to Company Y? Can @JoeBlogsCompanyX really just morph into @JoeBlogsCompanyY, sailing into the sunset along with all his followers and business contacts?

This was the case in 2011, when the BBC effectively lost almost 60 000 Twitter followers after political correspondent Laura Kuenssberg joined rival ITV. A few months before her departure, she tweeted from her *@BBCLauraK* account:

 As you've discovered I will become @ITVLauraK in September!

In 2013 in South Africa, a few months before he stepped down as CEO of FNB, Michael Jordaan tweeted:

 Please feel free to unfollow me and follow @CelliersJ1 and #Rbjacobs if you only followed ex officio

It was a magnificent pre-emptive strike, as the bank no doubt would have wanted to take over Jordaan's Twitter account, which had built up a mass following and had come to represent a highly regarded line of communication between FNB and its customers.

How much is a Twitter follower worth?

When Noah Kravitz left US mobile phone review website PhoneDog, he took 17 000 followers of his @PhoneDog_ Noah Twitter account (changed to @NoahKravitz) with him. PhoneDog wasn't impressed, claiming that his departure resulted in a loss in advertising revenue. They sued Kravitz for $340 000 (or $2.50 per follower per month), a number that may or may not have been sucked out of PhoneDog's thumb. The matter was eventually settled. Kravitz kept his account and his followers, and we'll never know how much they were deemed to be worth.

As far as the law is concerned, the status of social media contacts and followers is unfortunately far from certain. Technically, the account, and all the associated contacts, belongs to the person who operates it; yet social media accounts are the 21st-century rolodex, and there is certainly scope for an argument that an employer can stake a claim to contacts made in the course and scope of employment and arising as part of an employee's business operations.

135

- In 2008, a case was heard in the UK concerning an employee who, having left his job to start a rival business, was suspected of inviting former clients to join his LinkedIn network of contacts. The court sided with the employer, ordering the former employee to disclose the LinkedIn business contacts he had acquired during his employment, as well as all communications between his LinkedIn account and the employer's computer network during his employment.
- In the USA, the co-founder and former CEO of EdComm, Inc. was successful in her legal action against her former employer after they took over a LinkedIn account that she had set up and maintained (together with a colleague) to promote herself and the business. When her employment was terminated, EdComm changed the account password, and replaced her name and photograph with that of her successor, in such a way that those searching for her on LinkedIn were directed to the new CEO's information.

Although these cases give *some* insight into the status of employee social media accounts, it is far from clear how similar scenarios – involving LinkedIn contacts, Twitter followers or otherwise – would be dealt with in terms of South African law.

And that's all good and well, but 'No one knows!' is not a very helpful answer.

If companies do want to encourage employees to use social media to build their business, without a big grey question mark hanging over their exit, we'd recommend they be proactive and face the issue head-on. Although by no means foolproof, consider the following:

- Put a policy in place detailing how ownership of employee accounts is to be dealt with. Be clear in distinguishing between work and social contacts. Understand that social media often straddles the line between work and play, so be pragmatic.
- Introduce an obligation for exiting employees to delete and hand over details of all business contacts made during the course of employment.
- Consider requiring an employee to set up a *new* LinkedIn account upon joining the company, to be used solely for business purposes. Make it clear that all connections made with that account are proprietary trade information built on the employer's behalf. If the employee leaves, they will be required to hand over access to the account in full.
- Oblige employees who tweet in a professional or quasi-professional capacity to include a reference to the business in their Twitter handle. If the employer's intention is to retain ownership of the account after termination of the employment relationship, the employee must know this from the outset.
- Require all LinkedIn connections to be copied to the employer's main database – although note that in terms of POPI, the prior consent of the LinkedIn connection should be obtained before transferral can take place.
- Include reasonable restrictions on solicitation of clients via social media in your standard contract of employment.

CHAPTER 30

Occupational hazards

Managing platforms

The digital age is one of instant gratification. Consumers no longer want to drive to the local branch of the bank; they want an app for that. Consumers don't want to call customer services; they want to tweet their complaint (and expect an immediate answer). Social media allows brands to not only speak the same language as their consumers, but to increase accessibility to their products and services and monitor how their brand is perceived by the wider public.

As such, we are beginning to see more and more companies getting onto social media. And that's great, but in stepping onto the social media stage, companies expose themselves to a degree of legal and regulatory liability.

> Your company doesn't need to be on *every* platform. Rather do one platform right than overextend yourself. Understand your consumer, understand your message, and decide on the best platform to make your company's voice heard.

Liability for user-generated content

Judge Satchwell's 2012 ruling on the liability of the creator of a Facebook page (you might remember from Chapter 6 that the page was likened to a felt notice board, from which the page administrator had an obligation to remove unlawful postings) has significant ramifications for those companies that make use of Facebook, and other social media websites, to interact with consumers. By allowing the general public to comment and post content to your company-controlled page, you become responsible for all such content and commentary.

This is particularly problematic in instances where your social media presence spirals into a complaints forum and platform for abuse and hate speech, as was the case in 2012 when Woolworths elected to disable the wall on its Facebook page in the midst of public controversy surrounding its hiring practices. In a statement explaining their decision, Woolworths wrote:

> We have allowed thousands of comments on our Facebook page, debating the pros and cons of Employment Equity and deleted only overt hate speech and comments inciting violence. However, many customers have asked us to stop hosting this vitriol. We will re-open our page as soon as we think we can resume reasonable discussion.

> Twitter is a different beast, because you are not in control of what appears on your timeline. As you cannot delete third-party mentions on Twitter, you cannot be held legally responsible for replies or mentions.

Compliance with industry regulation

As noted earlier, companies are typically regulated by some kind of regulatory body or industry-specific code of conduct, be it the Financial Services Board, the Advertising Standards Authority of South Africa Code of Practice or otherwise. The rules dictated by these regulatory bodies and codes of conduct will naturally apply to the specific company's conduct online, whether on a website or social media.

It was on this basis that Swiss-based pharmaceutical company IBSA Institut Biochimique SA got into trouble with the US Food and Drug Administration (FDA), when it posted on its Facebook page:

 If you have just been diagnosed with hypothyroidism or are having difficulty controlling your levothyroxine blood levels, talk to your doctor about prescription Tirosint, a unique liquid gel cap form of levothyroxine

The statement was deemed to be in violation of federal regulation, since it made representations about the efficacy of a drug without communicating the concomitant risk information. Similarly, the FDA took issue with AMARC Enterprises in 2013 when it 'liked' a consumer testimonial about one of its products, as it amounted to the endorsement of an unauthorised drug claim.

Employer's guide to managing online platforms

► Put a set of Terms and Conditions in place for use of any social media platforms or website run by the company where the ability exists for third parties to post user-generated content. These should at the very least:
  ▷ Encourage users not to use the website as a complaints forum, by directing them to a specific telephone number or email address to which complaints should be sent.

▷ Set out a list of speech that is prohibited, including defamatory content, hate speech and speech that incites violence.
▷ Explain that comments in breach of the Terms and Conditions will be summarily removed.
▷ Allow for a mechanism for users to report a violation of the Terms and Conditions.
▶ Provided you have a mechanism for abuses to be reported, do not actively monitor the page. If you do come across anything genuinely objectionable, or are notified thereof, delete it immediately.
▶ Take screenshots of all content before deleting it, together with as much detail about the offending user as possible. Just in case.
▶ In instances where a website allows third parties to post comments, utilise a registration procedure that gathers as much identifying information about users as possible (within the constraints of POPI, of course).
▶ Staff or third-party agencies that are charged with managing the social media presence of the company must be well versed in the regulatory particularities of the industry.

> ### Social media in the boardroom
>
> In the digital age, board diversity is critical. Many of the issues that companies have with social media stem from a generational disconnect. The generation of digital citizens is innovative, connected and has a lot of ideas about bringing business into the 21st century – listen to them.

Don't blame it on the intern

Companies are usually really protective over the voice of their brand, and who gets to speak for them. This typically involves high-level sign-off of all print and television advertisements and the hiring of people with important-yet-horribly-vague-sounding titles like 'Communications Manager'.

Yet, despite social media being the go-to medium for brand engagement in the 21st century, companies seem less protective over their social media voice, and we've come across many high-profile organisations that outsource it to the first kid that looks like he vaguely knows what Twitter is.

This came back to haunt CNBC Africa in 2013, when it emerged that they had copied and pasted a series of tweets by its rival Business Day Television, passing them off as their own. CNBC Africa responded by admitting that copying had taken place, calling it an 'error in judgment' by a junior intern.

We have no reason to doubt that CNBC Africa's explanation was genuine, but it does evidence a wider phenomenon of companies reacting to social media faux pas by quickly declaring, 'It wasn't me!'

Luckily, we're slowly beginning to see this attitude change, as more and more entities cotton on to the fact that social media matters. In a noticeable shift from the blame-it-on-the-intern mentality of years past, the latest social media gaffes have seen the offending companies step up and take the rap.

In 2014, in response to a customer query on Twitter, the official account of US Airways tweeted:

 We welcome feedback, Elle. If your travel is complete, you can detail it here for review and follow-up: [hyperlink]

All perfectly fine, right?

Wrong.

Because the hyperlink did not navigate to a customer review mechanism, but rather to a *very* explicit picture involving a toy plane. Take our word for it and don't google it. And if you must, do it out of the sight of all children. And adults. And puppies. And anything else with eyes. #NSFW

Naturally, the tweet immediately went viral, prompting worldwide coverage and a grovelling apology from the airline.

Apparently, our very own First National Bank was not paying attention to the US Airways blunder, because only a few days later, in response to a customer enquiry as to the whereabouts of fictitious FNB spokesperson 'Steve', @RBJacobs (the official corporate presence of FNB on Twitter) responded:

 somewhere in Afghanistan, putting a bomb under a wheelchair and telling the cripple to run for it!

cue South Africans uniting in collective stunned silence

The incident made national news. FNB quickly deleted the tweet and apologised for any offence caused. Importantly, neither US Airways nor FNB resorted to finger-pointing or scapegoating. They took it on the chin – a strategy that, incidentally, appeared to elicit more support and sympathy than denigration.

Ultimately, brands need to accept that the voice on social media is often louder than anywhere else. As such, they need to invest appropriate time and resources into managing their voice on these platforms, whether through dedicated staff or by outsourcing their social media activity to one of the many agencies set up for that very purpose. Either way, this is not something to be handed over without a second thought: companies need to make sure that sufficient controls are in place to ensure that the right message is being sent. Companies also need to realise that social media is no longer just a marketing item: a company's online and social media presence must form part of an integrated risk management framework.

Mistakes do happen, certainly. But as consumers begin to demand more from the brands they engage with, it is no longer good enough to point the finger at the poor junior intern when the proverbial twit hits the fan.

PART V

THE CHILDREN BIT

CHAPTER 31

Generation Z

Introduction to a digital childhood

Every parent (and future parent) reading this book needs to accept one thing: your children's life will be forever entwined with digital technology. It will fundamentally impact the way they communicate, form relationships and conduct business. To your children, the Internet, social media and Web 2.0 (and Web 3.0 and Web 4.0 ...) are not the brave new world that you're busy navigating, but rather, all they know.

Your children will not know the joy of ignorance; the joy of waiting to get home to page through a dusty encyclopedia to find out more about ladybirds. Your children will not know the joy of forgetting; of moving on from their mistakes. Your children will not know the butterflies that come with having to pick up the phone to ask a girl out. Your children will know all about sex long before you sit down to talk about the birds and the bees. The conversations your children will have with their classmates will not take place on the playground or on a scrappy note changing hands in third-period Geography, but rather in front of the whole world. To your children, digital technology is like breathing.

The future of digital natives?

▶ Tablet computers are a reality of education in the digital age as more and more schools go paperless. Gone are the days of handwritten assignments. Or handwritten *anything*.

▶ Concerns have been raised that children who spend too much time online find it harder to concentrate in class, are permanently distracted and have worryingly short attention spans.

▶ Schools around the world have seen a rise in 'text-speak' in their class work and assignments. *2moro*, *u*, *msg* and *gud* are just some of the culprits.

Once you have accepted the reality that your children are faced with, accept that you have to take the time *now* to teach them about online responsibility. Accept that your children will spend the rest of their lives having to navigate each and every risk we've outlined in this book – from identity fraud to malicious impersonation – as well as a number of risks unique to them as children. Accept that, in the digital age, not only do you have to teach your kids to clean their room, do their homework, eat their broccoli and not do drugs, but you also have to teach them about the importance of online safety. Accept that it is only through instilling an understanding and appreciation of the dangers of digital technology that you allow your children to truly reap its benefits.

We are not parents, psychologists or teachers, and have no doubt that you know what is best for you and your family. But in our line of work, we have been exposed to some horror stories in terms of what children have to endure online every day. So to help you in guiding your children through the digital age, we will outline in the chapters to follow what we consider to be the five key risks facing your child in the digital era, together with some tips to help you in educating and protecting them.

The most important advice we can give you is to take an active interest in your children's online life. Have sympathy for the uncertainty and added pressure that come with having to go through adolescence in the digital age. Talk to them about what they are doing. Build a sense of trust and understanding, without blame or judgement, so that you are the one they turn to if they find themselves in trouble. And please, teach them about proper spelling and grammar – *ppl who tlk lik thiz r bound 2 fail @ life, lol.*

CHAPTER 32

No clue what your kids are saying?

A guide to the secret language of digital natives

In no way should any of the below be construed or interpreted as our endorsement or support of the use of these ridiculous 'words'. In fact, we're hoping that this book will help to eradicate them.

@	at
<3	heart
2day	today
2moro	tomorrow
2nite	tonight
4eva	forever
ab/abt	about
atm	at the moment
b4	before
b/c	because
bf	boyfriend or best friend
bff	best friend forever
brb	be right back
btw	by the way
cud/cld	could
DM	direct message
dtf	down (willing) to fuck
f2f/ftf	face to face
FB	Facebook
#FF	Friday Follow – used on Twitter on Fridays to indicate people that they think others should follow
ffs	for fuck sake

fomo	fear of missing out (as in, 'I'm having real FOMO')
ftw	for the win (the best, great, awesome)
fyi	for your information
gf	girlfriend
gr8	great
gtfo	get the fuck out
h8	hate
idk	I don't know
jk	just kidding
l8r	later
lmao/lmfao	laughing my ass off/laughing my fucking ass off
lol	laughing out loud
meh	who cares / whatever
mofo	motherfucker
msg	message
mwah/muah	kiss
nm	never mind
NSFW	not safe for work (usually referring to a link containing explicit content that you should not be accessing at your desk)
obvs	obviously
omg/omfg	oh my God/oh my fucking God
orly	oh really?
peeps	people
pls/plz	please
ppl	people
rofl	rolling on the floor laughing
RT	retweet
sm1	someone
smt/sth	something
soz/sry	sorry
srsly	seriously
stfu	shut the fuck up
thx/tk/tx	thank you
TMI	too much information (typically with reference to over-sharing of intimate details of one's life)
tmrw	tomorrow
Twtr	Twitter
txt	text

ur	you are/your
w/e	weekend
wtf	what the fuck
YOLO	you only live once
zomg	oh my God (used sarcastically)

Just a kid?

Your sweet innocent little angel can still get into some serious legal trouble

In South Africa, you attain majority at the age of 18. That means that you're an adult, and get to do awesome adult things like drink and drive (not at the same time, obvs!).

But the law also has this concept called *capacity*. If you have capacity, you can be held legally responsible for the things you do. And just because you're not an adult, doesn't mean that you don't have capacity and cannot be held responsible for your actions.

The question is at what age someone attains this capacity. All the under-18s are hoping that the answer is 18, right? Or 21? Or 40? Hoping that they get to run wild for a little longer ...

When does a child have capacity to enter into binding contracts?

The Children's Act 2005 provides as follows:

▶ In general, contractual capacity is acquired at 18.
▶ *But* a child under the age of 18 does have contractual capacity in respect of contracts that grant only rights without any obligations (show us one of those, they sound awesome!).
▶ *And* a child under the age of 18 can enter into a contract in respect of which he or she acquires both rights and responsibilities, if assisted or represented by a parent or guardian.

So what does this mean? By signing up to any social media website, a user is essentially entering into a contractual relationship with the company that operates that website and agreeing to be bound by their terms and conditions. If that user is under the age of 18, they do not have contractual capacity, so if a dispute were to ever arise, the user is unlikely to be held to the terms of the contract.

Off the hook? Not so fast!

If a parent either consents to their child being on the given website, or finds out that they are signed up and does nothing about it, the parent may well be held to have tacitly consented to their child's contract with the website.

When does a child have capacity to commit a crime?

Here's another Act for you (sorry!). In terms of the Child Justice Act 2008:

▶ A child under the age of 10 does not have capacity to commit a crime and can therefore never be prosecuted. If a three-year-old child picks up a gun, shoots someone and that person then dies, the child cannot be charged with murder. This is because a child under the age of 10 doesn't have criminal *capacity* and therefore, in the eyes of the law, does not know right from wrong.
▶ A child over the age of 10 and under the age of 14 is *presumed* not to have criminal capacity. However, if it can be shown that the child can appreciate the difference between right and wrong, and is able to act in accordance with that appreciation, the child will be held to have criminal capacity.
▶ A child over the age of 14 has full criminal capacity and can be prosecuted for any offence that he or she commits.

Under 10	Over 10 but under 14	Over 14
No criminal capacity	May have criminal capacity	Full criminal capacity

When does a child have capacity to be sued in civil proceedings?

Let's start by first understanding what it means to be sued in civil proceedings. Civil law is non-criminal law. So to be sued in civil proceedings is to be sued by someone (for example for defamation, a breach of privacy or a breach of copyright) as opposed to being prosecuted by the State for a crime (for example theft, assault or murder).

▶ A child under the age of seven may be sued, but in the name of the child's parent (sorry, Mum and Dad!) or a curator appointed by the court to look after the child.
▶ A child between the ages of seven and 18 may be sued in their own name, although they of course have the right to legal representation, which includes the right to have a curator or separate legal representative appointed. Court papers must be served on the child's parent, guardian or curator.
▶ Once you're over 18, you have full capacity to sue and be sued in your own name.

Under 7	Over 7 but under 18	Over 18
Sued in the name of parent or guardian	Sued in own name, with assistance of parent or guardian	Full litigation capacity

Now if you're sitting there thinking that no one in his or her right mind would sue a child, take heed of this story:

One Sunday morning in 2006, a 15-year-old boy was at home in Pretoria, surfing the Internet. On his school's website, he came across a picture of the principal and deputy principal. Thinking back to an episode of *South Park*, he thought it would be super-duper funny to Photoshop the heads of his principal and deputy principal onto the bodies of gay bodybuilders. So he trawled through the web and managed to find a picture of two naked men sitting next to each other in a sexually suggestive position, and proceeded to transpose the faces of his principal and deputy principal onto the picture. As the cherry on top, he transposed a picture of his school badge over the men's genitals.

He presumably thought this was hilarious and, as with all hilarious things, he sent the doctored image to his friend. Lol.

At church later that day, he met his friend and implored him not to distribute the image. Despite his pleas, through the magic of mobile technology mixed with a little bit of schoolboy mischief, the image was widely circulated and – lo and behold! – ended up on the school notice board.

The school authorities were not impressed. Obviously.

As punishment, the boys involved were not allowed to assume leadership positions at the school, or wear honorary colours, for the remainder of the school year. They also had to sit in detention for a total of 15 hours.

But that wasn't enough. The deputy principal laid criminal charges against the boys, and they ended up having to perform community service by cleaning cages at a local zoo.

But that still wasn't enough. The deputy principal also sued the boys for R600 000, on account of injury to his dignity, good name and reputation.

The matter was heard by the High Court and the Supreme Court of Appeal and eventually ended up before the Constitutional Court – the very highest court in all of the land. The ConCourt (we like to abbreviate it because we think it makes us sound cool) held that the vision created by the boys was defamatory, as it would be embarrassing and disgraceful to ordinary members of society.

The boys were ordered to pay the deputy principal R25 000, together with an unconditional apology. They were also ordered to pay the deputy principal's costs in the High Court (and if you know anything about lawyers, you'll know that they're not exactly cheap ...)

So you see, that little joke that your kid makes on social media, online or anywhere else could actually land them in court. Or in jail. It doesn't matter how old they are. And we're going to hazard a guess and say that if Mum and Dad have to pay hundreds of thousands of rands to get their child out of trouble, that kid is going to be grounded for a really, really, *really* long time.

CHAPTER 34

You know that dodgy guy who used to hand out free candy outside the school gates? He's gone digital too

Online predators

Parents are very good at teaching children not to talk to strangers. From a young age, kids know not to accept anything from someone they don't know – whether it's a chocolate, a gift or a lift home. They are taught to be wary of lone men hanging around playgrounds, and not to walk home alone. They know to tell someone if they are made to feel uncomfortable by an adult. After all, it is the responsibility of parents to protect their children from predators.

But protecting your children from 'real-world' predators is no longer good enough. Because in the digital age, it is far more likely that a child will come across a predator in cyberspace than in the street. And in the digital age, predators come in many guises. While your child probably knows to avoid the guy outside school selling candy out of his beaten-up old van, or the hooded figure lurking in the shadows, a recent experiment conducted by the principal of a Pretoria high school has shown that children are not as cautious when it comes to their online interactions. Posing as a pretty 16-year-old girl on Facebook, more than 100 of the school's pupils accepted 'her' friend request, despite obviously never having met her. Luckily for all involved, no one came to any harm. But that friendly girl from the neighbouring school who adds your child as a friend on Facebook could well be a violent predator. The good-looking guy that strikes up a conversation in a chatroom? He could be a predator. Potentially every single person your child comes across online could be a predator. In fact, the FBI has estimated that there are 750 000 child predators connected to the Internet at any given moment.

So really, as a parent, you can no longer dismiss social media as something for the kids. Because while you're busy protecting them from that lone figure outside the playground, your child is potentially coming 'face to face' with him online.

Protecting your children from online predators

Here are some guidelines on how you can help your children avoid predators operating online.

Educate yourself

▶ Learn more about the websites and applications your children are using. For you to be truly aware of the dangers your children face online, you need to have an understanding of how these platforms work.
▶ Read the privacy policy of the websites your children are using. Be particularly cautious of websites that use your children's content for commercial purposes.

Teach your children to value and guard their personal information

▶ Set up ground rules for the sharing of personal information. However innocuous it seems, children should only share their personal information (such as a phone number, address and date of birth) with people approved by you.
▶ Work with your child in setting up their social media accounts. Make sure that they have implemented strong privacy settings, including any setting that allows for comments, photographs and other content to be pre-approved.
▶ Children must never share the login details or password to any of their online accounts with anyone (except you).
▶ Turn off GPS 'check-ins' that identify the location of your children's mobile devices.
▶ Sometimes social media and other online websites will ask children to list personal information such as their full name, city, school and age. Remind them that this information should not be made public.
▶ Personal information can be accidentally revealed in text and images uploaded online. Teach your children to think before they post, and carefully consider whether what they're about to do will expose private information.

Not everyone in cyberspace is who they say they are

▶ Instil a sense of caution: children should beware of anyone they don't know trying to join their network of friends. Even if the person is friends with their friends, or seems to know things about your child, they must know to *never* interact with anyone online who they have not met in the real world.
▶ Most social networks have a mechanism to report incidences that breach the terms and conditions of the website, as well as the ability to block users. Ensure that your child knows how to use these handy tools.
▶ Children must never ever meet face to face with someone they first met online.

Let them know that they can speak up

▶ Encourage your children to tell you if someone online ever makes them feel threatened or uncomfortable. Children need to know that it is never too late to tell someone.
▶ Speak to your children about sexual victimisation.
▶ Highlight the importance of trusting their gut. If something seems suspicious, it probably is.

Technology exists to protect your children. Use it

▶ Consider installing software that blocks outgoing transmissions of personal information.
▶ Install tracking software on your child's phone or tablet. Ask your service provider about a paid service such as Cellfind, otherwise activate one of the free services offered on BlackBerry, Samsung, Android and Apple devices. Some smartphones also allow for a digital 'panic button' to be activated.

Engage with other parents

▶ Many times, it is friends who facilitate the introduction of dubious characters. It is therefore not even enough to teach your own child about online safety – you need to ensure that your child's friends are being made aware of the same risks, and know not to share your child's personal information with third parties.
▶ Consider setting up a parents' meeting or training session at your school to facilitate discussion amongst parents.

CHAPTER 35

Tweeting your way to expulsion

Social media and schools

If you're a parent, we're presuming that, having read all about how you can lose your job because of something you said or did online, you had a minor panic attack and ran off immediately to delete any references to your employer from your social media accounts. But you probably didn't worry too much about your children. After all, they have a few more years before they have to worry about their online conduct bringing about any serious disciplinary consequences at their job.

But, just like you and your employer, the relationship a learner has with his or her school is also a contractual one. As is required by the Schools Act 1996, each student is bound by a Code of Conduct, setting out a whole list of what is considered to be unacceptable behaviour and requiring pupils not to bring the school into disrepute. This learner Code of Conduct typically applies to all activities on campus or during school hours and, in almost every one we've ever come across, to the extent that a child can be identified as a pupil of the school.

Now when we were at school, we knew that we had to be on our best behaviour on campus, on school tour and walking around the shops in our school uniform. But we could rest easy in the knowledge that as soon as we were outside the school gates and took off our uniform, we were pretty much free to do what we wanted. What went on on a Saturday night was our business, and had nothing to do with what happened in the classroom from Monday to Friday.

Schoolchildren these days have an entirely different set of circumstances to contend with, because the Internet transcends the distinction between school and play. The permanence and reach of social media mean that what goes on on a Saturday night is no longer 'outside of school hours'. It's on Instagram on Monday morning, passed around amongst friends in the hallways. To make matters even trickier, the ability to identify learners as a student of their school is also far greater online: listing their school on their social media profile, liking a school page and being friends with fellow pupils all work together to build a profile of a child as a student of a particular school.

Therefore, if a learner's online conduct or social media posts are deemed to be in breach of the Code of Conduct to which he or she is bound as a pupil of the school, or in any way damages the reputation of the school, that learner can be disciplined and, in serious cases, expelled.

Uh ... what code of conduct?

If you're wondering what on earth we're talking about, the school Code of Conduct is that long document that they handed to your child at the beginning of the school year, and which they stuffed into their suitcase without reading. Or what your child handed you at the beginning of the school year, and which you stuffed into your desk drawer without reading.

Pleading ignorance, however, is not necessarily enough to get them off the hook, as most schools require some or other signature confirming that the Code of Conduct and other school policies have been read and understood.

Yeah, yeah – schools are all talk and no action

What are the chances that a school is *actually* going to discipline your child because of something they said online?

Pretty high actually. As endless pupils in South Africa have recently found out. We won't list them all, but here are just a few case studies to scare you:

▶ In Port Elizabeth, a Matric student was stripped of his prefect badge and tie after tweeting about a drinking spree. After taking the decision on review, a court ruled that the school had not acted unreasonably.
▶ A Johannesburg Matric student faced a disciplinary hearing, and narrowly avoided expulsion, for tweeting something vulgar and derogatory about a female pupil.
▶ Having started a parody account in the name of a teacher, a Matric student was disciplined and threatened with expulsion.
(Seriously, Matrics? Get it together.)
▶ A pupil at a private Johannesburg school was expelled for a violent rant about the school on Facebook.
▶ A Grade 11 student was summarily expelled after tweeting a link to a porn site. She made no mention of her school in her Twitter profile, and did not tweet under her full name.

Children need to understand that the disciplinary consequences of getting it wrong online could be very serious indeed. Posting a photograph, status or comment on social media is just like sticking that photograph, status or comment on their school locker, and their school has every right to discipline them accordingly. Even more so, that photograph, status or comment could also seriously jeopardise a child's future university placement and job prospects.

Yes, it sucks. Yes, life is so unfair. Yes, maybe a bit of a tantrum is warranted. But this is, unfortunately, another reality of growing up in the 21st century.

CHAPTER 36

See no evil

The exposure of children to inappropriate material online

From graphic images, explicit videos and hate speech, to obscenity and gratuitous violence, the Internet has it all. Perfectly legal, but certainly not meant for children's eyes. And just like you don't let your 12-year-old rent movies with an age restriction of 18, or go to a drug-fuelled party, you have a responsibility as a parent to limit your child's exposure to adult content.

But can you really protect your child from objectionable content online? Well, yes and no.

You can start by adopting some of these readily available technological tools:

▶ Many of the operating systems that you already have on your computer have basic filtering tools that you can activate to block certain content and track usage.
▶ Google allows you to filter out explicit search results via the 'Search Settings' function.
▶ By contacting your service provider, you are easily able to block pornography on your child's smartphone or tablet, or disable the Internet completely.
▶ YouTube's content filter blocks objectionable videos, while still allowing your children to enjoy the site's appropriate content.
▶ Apps such as K9, SmyleSafe, MobiCip and KytePhone allow for safer browsing of the web on tablets and smartphones.

> Remember that your child is not only accessing the web on devices supplied by you. So take steps to ensure that your child's school has appropriate blocking and filtering software installed on all school-issued devices.

Once you have those in place, the best way to minimise unwanted material on devices to which your children have access is to install some kind of specialised filtering software. There are loads of options for you to choose from to block out graphic images, offensive language and inappropriate content. Here are some features to look out for:

▶ *Web blocking* prevents your children from viewing inappropriate content.
▶ *Program blocking* blocks games, peer-to-peer file sharing, and other harmful programs.
▶ *Email blocking* blocks mail from unknown email addresses, and also allows you to prevent personal information being sent from your child's address.
▶ *Instant Message features* monitor and record instant messaging (IM) chats to help spot inappropriate dialogue.
▶ *Online usage reports* provide you with a complete view of all Internet and IM activity.
▶ You can set up *alerts* to notify you when your children attempt to access something not meant for innocent eyes.

As a last resort, don't shy away from monitoring your children's online usage, especially if they have the ability to access the Internet and social media from a young age. Yes, they'll probably tell you that they hate you, slam their bedroom door and sulk for a few days. But they'll get over it.

In throwing a tantrum, what they fail to see is that, as much as they think otherwise, a teenager does not have the emotional maturity to face the digital world without a nurturing parental hand to guide them. The fact is that we live in an age in which innocence is all too easily lost. Parents therefore need to fight for their children's right to be just that: a *child*.

What about privacy?

We do understand that you may be feeling a little uncomfortable about all this. And we get it. Many of these measures are controversial and perhaps a little too Big Brother-ish for your liking.

As we're sure your child will be very quick to point out (hopefully because they were paying attention in Chapter 7), he or she does have a right to privacy.

But *you* also have a responsibility to keep your child safe.

You'll remember how we told you all about how the test for privacy in South Africa is whether the subject has a reasonable expectation of privacy in those circumstances. In our view, a child afforded the privilege of using a device supplied by their parent, in their parent's home, using their parent's network, doesn't have any such reasonable expectation of privacy. And even if they do, there is a strong public interest argument in not letting your 12-year-old run amok with access to hardcore pornography and sites depicting gratuitous violence. Sorry, kids, in this instance, safety trumps privacy.

So if you have a reasonable suspicion that they're up to something, feel free to start monitoring your children's Internet usage. But don't use this, or any other technological measures that you implement, as an excuse not to engage in an open and frank discussion with your kids about what they're being exposed to online. Continue to educate them about the dangers of the web. Make sure they understand that their laptop/desktop/tablet/smartphone is a privilege, not a right. Explain to them that trust is not an entitlement, but something that is earned. And hopefully, through a combination of old-fashioned conversation and 21st-century technology, you can sleep a little sounder at night.

But wait!

Before you get too comfortable and curl up for a good night's rest, we should just tell you that all this might actually be a moot point. Because the fact is that the nature of the interconnected world that we live in means that your children *will* come across unsuitable content. You can install as much filtering and security software as you want, and you can monitor their Internet usage until you're blue in the face, but just like two naughty boys coming across a discarded *Playboy* and giggling behind the bike shed, children will always get up to mischief. In particular, there is nothing you can do to stop what is known as 'peer-to-peer' content (friends sharing content amongst each other). You will, unfortunately, never be able to control every experience and conversation your children will have online.

So what is a parent to do? In the end, you can only hope that, whatever they come across, your kids will remain true to the values of online safety that you have instilled in them; that they will have enough common sense to avoid undesirable content; and that they will make responsible choices in the way they conduct themselves online.

Innocence lost

Underage sexual offences

Children are more connected than ever. No longer now restricted by clunky cellphones with limited functionality, smartphones now allow for the instant sharing of high-resolution photographs, while web-based instant messaging platforms mean that lengthy messages can be sent back and forth at no cost.

The ease and immediacy of these connections have bred a new trend amongst adolescents: sexting – the sending of sexually explicit messages, photos or videos, typically between cellphones and primarily for personal use (in case you hadn't figured it out by now, 'sexting' is a portmanteau of the words 'sex' and 'texting').

> One of the most popular apps amongst teens, SnapChat, allows users to send photos and videos to a controlled list of recipients, to be viewed for between one and 10 seconds before they 'disappear'. You can only imagine what sorts of images and videos some young children are sending to each other thinking that they are being deleted. But they're not deleted. Not only can a screenshot easily be taken, but the content is in fact just *hidden*, to be easily retrieved using apps such as SnapHack. SnapChat has reported that, as of May 2014, 700 million photos and videos are sent using the app every single day.

Now we fully appreciate that teenage curiosity and sexual exploration has been going on since long before smartphones. But the creation and sharing of sexual content on a permanent, public platform has thrown this phenomenon into uncharted – and deeply concerning – territory. No longer are children kissing behind the Wendy house or sneaking a peak at a naughty magazine; they're exposing themselves to the permanent reputational harm associated with revenge porn, as well as risks of extortion and public humiliation. Scary, yes, but by far the scariest part is that by engaging in sexting, your child is also committing a very serious crime.

You heard us: *crime*. All of a sudden, your teenager spending all his or her time on their phone chatting to their boyfriend or girlfriend becomes a whole lot more terrifying ...

Sexual offences in the digital age

In terms of the Films and Publications Act 1996, anything to do with child pornography is a crime. 'Child pornography' includes:

▶ Any *image*, however created; or
▶ any *description* of a person, real or simulated;
▶ who is, or who is depicted, made to appear, look like, represented or described as being *under the age of 18 years*;
▶ *engaged* in sexual conduct; or
▶ *participating* in, or assisting another person to participate in, sexual conduct; or
▶ *showing* or *describing* the body, or parts of the body, of such a person in a manner or in circumstances which, within context, amounts to *sexual exploitation*, or in such a manner that it is capable of being used for the purposes of sexual exploitation.

Whether you're in possession of it, encouraging it, creating it, procuring it, accessing it, making it available to someone or distributing it, you are a criminal. Whether it's a written description, a drawing, a photograph, a sound recording or some kind of electronic communication, it's a crime.

While the primary purpose of the law prohibiting child pornography is to criminalise the sexual abuse and exploitation of children, the net result – perhaps inadvertently – is that teenagers who engage in consensual sexting are guilty of an offence. What this means is that if someone under the age of 18 does any of the following, he or she has committed a criminal offence, with no defence available:

▶ takes a sexually explicit picture of him- or herself;
▶ sends sexually explicit pictures of him- or herself;
▶ has a sexually explicit picture of him- or herself or another teen on their phone or computer; or
▶ *asks* an under-18 to send a sexually explicit picture.

The Films and Publications Act further *obliges* any person who has knowledge or suspicion that a child pornography offence has been committed to inform the police, failing which he or she will be guilty of an offence. In simpler terms, parents, educators, social workers and psychologists who become aware of any sexting, whether consensual or not, have no choice but to report the matter to the police.

And it doesn't end there. Because the Criminal Law (Sexual Offences and Related Matters) Amendment Act 2007 sets out even more offences related to pornography and children. Amongst these, it is an offence to expose or display pornography to a child. The definition of pornography is so long and expansive that we would never put you through having to read the whole thing (you're welcome) – basically, it's any explicit or sexual content that is intended to stimulate erotic feelings.

The person depicted in any pornographic pictures, videos or messages sent or shown to a child need therefore not be under the age of 18 in order for an offence to have been committed. The exposure of a child to *any* pornography is an offence.

Stepping up: Authorities around the world are taking underage sexting seriously

The laws on child pornography are relatively consistent throughout the world – it is actually the one thing that everyone seems to agree on – and there have been numerous convictions of teenagers worldwide on the basis of 'sexting-related' child pornography offences.

▶ In South Africa, a 17-year-old was convicted of manufacturing and distributing child pornography and given a three-year suspended prison sentence after sending naked selfies to a 42-year-old man. The matter was brought to the attention of the police when the girl's father found explicit messages and photographs on her phone and turned them over.
▶ In 2007, 32 Australian teenagers were charged with child pornography offences and placed on the sex offenders list on account of having explicit photographs of other teenagers on their computers and phones.
▶ In Canada, a 17-year-old girl was found guilty of possessing and distributing child pornography after sending nude pictures of her boyfriend's ex to a friend and posting one such picture on Facebook.
▶ In Florida, USA, when a 15-year-old girl was found to have sent a topless photo of herself to a boy of the same age, both were arrested and charged with transmission of pornography by electronic device.
▶ Again in the USA, police recently busted a 'sexting ring' involving more than 100 teens and over 1 000 photos of underage girls posted on Instagram.

To cut a very long story short, by engaging in consensual sexting, teenagers are committing a crime that is not going to be treated lightly. So before your children pick up their phone to engage in a bit of innocent flirtation, they need to imagine living the rest of their life with a conviction for creating or possessing child pornography (which is just about the worst thing that you could ever have on your record). It doesn't matter that it resulted from engaging in a bit of racy banter with a boyfriend or girlfriend. Your child will never escape a child pornography conviction.

Beware of posting intimate images or videos of children online

The age of social media is an age of sharing. It is an age in which we let the world in, sharing our experiences, the things that make us laugh and the people who are important to us. One way in which this desire to share our lives with the world manifests is through the posting online of intimate photographs of our life, and in particular, the children in our life: the cute picture of a toddler waddling down the beach without a nappy, siblings splashing around in the bath, or professional photo shoots showing day-old babies curled up in a ball with a flower on their head.

But be warned: in June 2014, the National Prosecuting Authority (NPA) issued a statement saying that the posting on social media of *any* kind of naked picture of a child is a criminal offence, and will be treated as a form of child pornography. In particular, it was stated that:

> [it's] irrelevant what the purpose was for taking the picture. But any image of a naked child is child pornography and the reason for that is quite simple; it can be abused. What you do innocently, others take and they abuse it.

Now, in our view, this is an overly strict application of the law relating to child pornography that is out of touch with reality. But, it doesn't really matter what we think. The fact is that our prosecuting authority has come out strongly against the sharing of pictures of naked children – however innocent, and whatever the intent behind them – on social media, and you may therefore be prosecuted for doing so.

Whether or not we agree with the approach that these images constitute child pornography, the NPA's statement does also highlight a few non-legal concerns around the practice of posting pictures of naked children on social media, particularly more explicit imagery in which genitals are shown. Firstly, we've discussed how the Internet never forgets, and how an online profile built up over time stays with an individual through their life and career. Where children are too young to make decisions about their own bodies, and cannot speak up for themselves about how they wish to manage their online profile and image, is it really your place as a parent to share such personal images of them online, for all the world to see?

But most importantly, the relative innocence of the images does not change the fact that there are some depraved individuals operating online. Of course, for the majority of the population, pictures of children elicit nothing more than an 'Aw, cute!' and represent a harmless moment captured in the life of a child. Unfortunately, for some, these pictures elicit something infinitely more sinister. Although not 'child pornography' in the traditional sense, a broader category of what is known as 'child sexual abuse imagery' may still contribute to the violation and degradation of the child depicted. Knowing what you know about online predation and the horrifying numbers of people trawling the web every day in an attempt to find pictures or videos to satisfy their sick desires, is it really worth exposing your child to this risk for the sake of a few likes?

Tips for parents

▶ Make your kids read this chapter. We wish it was scaremongering, but it's all true.

▶ Encourage your children to come to you if they are feeling pressured to engage in sexting.

▶ Recognise the courage and maturity that it takes for a child to tell you about sexting – and never judge.

▶ Don't immediately ban your children from the Internet, or take away their phone, if they do come to you. This will only discourage openness and honesty.

▶ Think before posting any image or video of a child without clothes on, and in particular any image or video in which genitals are revealed. Take heed of the NPA's warning and, most importantly, beware that in doing so, there is a risk that the content is misappropriated by online predators. As innocent as the intent behind the imagery is, ask yourself if it could be abused should it land up in a dark corner of the Internet, viewed by a depraved individual.

CHAPTER 38

The scourge of 24/7 torment

Cyberbullying and the online harassment of children

From pulling pigtails in the playground to vicious name-calling, bullying has existed since time in memoriam. But just as with every other aspect of modern life, technology has put a spin on traditional bullying. A really ugly spin.

Whereas bullying has historically been restricted to the school campus, digital technology means that bullying can now happen any time – day or night – and can be carried out entirely anonymously. Bullying no longer stops when the school bell rings. It follows children home from school, to the dinner table, to their bedroom. Bullying is no longer restricted to victimisation in front of a handful of classmates. It spreads like a virus, beyond the walls of any classroom or school, with little risk of intervention. The extent of the bullying is also so much worse, as children can now hide behind a screen, unaffected by the real-time emotional consequences of their hurtful, barbed words. They feel empowered in the worst possible sense. They have the ability to be more hateful and more extreme than they could ever be in the real world.

This is not traditional bullying. This is cyberbullying: the harassment, abuse and victimisation of children online and on social media. It has become a worrying epidemic, with the intensity, rapid spread and all-consuming nature of cyberbullying resulting in all-too-many young children taking their own lives.

▶ **Megan Meier** When 13-year-old Megan Meier opened a MySpace account, she began innocently exchanging friendly messages with a 16-year-old boy called Josh Evans. However, the tone of the messages eventually changed, with 'Josh' sharing some of Megan's messages and posting abusive bulletins about her.

  In 2006, Megan was found hanged in her bedroom cupboard 20 minutes after sending 'Josh' a message saying, 'You're the kind of boy a girl would kill herself over.'

  Lori Drew, the mother of Megan's former friend, later admitted to creating the 'Josh Evans' MySpace account in order to humiliate

Megan. Megan's death resulted in several jurisdictions in the USA enacting legislation prohibiting harassment over the Internet.

▶ **Rehtaeh Parsons** In 2011, 15-year-old Canadian Rehtaeh Parsons was allegedly sexually assaulted by four boys at a house party. When a photograph of the incident was widely circulated within Rehtaeh's school and hometown, Parsons was branded a 'slut', and received texts and Facebook messages from people asking her for sex.

In April 2013, Rehtaeh hanged herself in her home. After three days in a coma, a decision was made to turn off her life-support machine. In the aftermath of her suicide, an 18-year-old boy was charged with distributing child pornography, while another was charged with creating and distributing child pornography. Rehtaeh's death also led to Nova Scotia passing a new law allowing victims to take out protection orders against, and sue, the perpetrator of cyberbullying.

▶ **Audrie Pott** In a similar incident, 15-year-old Californian Audrie Pott was bullied after pictures of her sexual assault – which occurred at a house party in 2012 after Audrie had passed out – were widely distributed via social media and SMS. In the aftermath, Audrie wrote on Facebook that her life was over, and that she had 'a reputation for a night I don't even remember, and the whole school knows'. Eight days after the assault, Audrie hanged herself.

▶ **Amanda Todd** Also in 2012, 15-year-old Amanda Todd posted a heartbreaking video on YouTube, entitled 'My Story: Struggling, bullying, suicide and self-harm'. In it, she detailed the anxiety, depression, abuse and humiliation that followed an incident years earlier when she was coerced into flashing her breasts to a man in an online chatroom. When she refused his demands to do so again, the man created a Facebook profile with the partially nude photo as the profile picture and used it to contact classmates at her school.

A month after posting the video, Amanda hanged herself in her home. More than a year passed before a Dutch man was arrested in connection with Amanda's death. He is alleged to have enticed many underage girls to perform sexual acts via a webcam, while surreptitiously filming them, and then using the footage to threaten and coerce them to perform even more explicit acts. The investigation and potential extradition of the man to the USA is ongoing. As of May 2014, Amanda's video had received nearly 18 million views.

▶ **Viviana Aguirre** Having recently broken up with her boyfriend, a young Italian girl calling herself 'Amnesia' sought comfort from users on the social network Ask.com. But instead of sympathy, the 14-year-old began receiving messages telling her that she was worthless, that nobody would miss her and encouraging her to kill herself. In 2014, shortly after posting a tragic farewell on Facebook, Viviana jumped to her death from a high-rise building.

[**Childline** 0800 055 555]

Cyberbullying and the law

Obviously, bullying can be exceptionally harmful and traumatic, and the effects are only amplified in the digital era. What victims of cyberbullying should not lose sight of, however, is that the law can – and will – protect them. The Protection from Harassment Act 2011 (see Chapter 10) is an incredibly effective piece of legislation that operates to protect those who are victimised online. Children do not need the assistance of an adult in order to apply for a protection order under the Act. Criminal charges of *crimen injuria* or extortion could also be laid against the perpetrator of cyberbullying. And criminal charges mean *jail*.

Practical steps to protect your child

▶ Teach your child to take screenshots of abusive messages.
▶ Set up a Google Alert in the name of your child. This will allow you to monitor what is being said about them online.
▶ Social media websites have mechanisms to report bullying or harassment and to block abusive users. Just in case your child feels uncomfortable coming to you, educate them about these readily available tools.
▶ Serious threats should be reported to the police and/or your child's school.
▶ Remind your child that, although they may think it is funny, they could get into serious trouble if they log into someone else's account or use someone else's phone to post stupid, offensive or harassing messages, tweets or status updates.
▶ Clues from the real world can help piece together what is going on in the digital world. Pay attention to any stories of nastiness at school, as this bullying has the potential to extend into cyberspace.

CHAPTER 39

Leaving your kids to their own devices

Device management and the need to strike a healthy balance

If the preceding chapters have taught you anything, it's that the risks associated with your children engaging with digital technology on a daily basis should not be taken lightly. But aside from the safety and disciplinary risks, the very fact that children are engaging with digital technology all day every day is cause for concern in itself.

With access to tablets, smartphones and laptops, children know nothing else than to be constantly tapped in to a network of information and friends. Digital life is, in a word, inescapable. Now, as we said upfront, we are not psychologists, but there is an almost visceral reaction to the thought of children constantly plugged into cyberspace, never having a chance to step out from under the glow of their device, and never having the need to engage in a real human interaction.

> Although not officially recognised as an addiction, some suggest that the dopamine jolts brought about by online and social media interaction fuel obsessive compulsive behaviour.

Recent research suggests that overexposure to technologies – including cellphones, Internet and tablets – is associated with attention deficit disorders, cognitive delays, impaired learning, literacy issues, increased impulsivity and mental illness. Without parental supervision of technology use, it is further reported that children are sleep deprived to the point that their grades are detrimentally impacted.

Implementing device management

We are strong advocates of parents exercising a little practical device management. If you'd like to avoid your children becoming over-reliant on digital technologies, but rather want to promote a healthy digital life, consider implementing some of the following guiding principles in your home:

Manage time spent online

Set time limits for being online in a single sitting, and implement a nightly cut-off time. If you don't think that house rules will do the job, there is software available to limit the length of time spent connected to the Internet.

The American Academy of Pediatrics and the Canadian Society of Pediatrics advise that:

▶ infants aged 0–2 years should have no exposure to technology;
▶ children aged 3–5 years should be restricted to one hour per day;
▶ children aged 6–18 years should be restricted to 2 hours per day.

Let us know how it goes getting that to fly with your 17-year-old …

Keep tabs on your children's use of devices after dark

Don't allow your children to sleep with a device next to their bed. Not only does this lead to 'bored browsing', but it prevents them from being kept up late at night in conversation with friends. In a world where they are constantly connected, there is immeasurable benefit in your children removing themselves from the anxiety and stress of non-stop communication. A great way to implement this is to have a family charging station, where each family member can charge their device overnight, outside of their bedroom.

CHAPTER 40

Responsible digital citizenship is the new drugs talk

The time is now

As a parent, you might be feeling a little overwhelmed at this point.

We've said it before and we'll say it again: we feel desperately sorry for children growing up in the digital age, because it comes with a whole laundry list of extra risks and responsibilities. But we really don't want all this talk of the dangers facing children online to scare you too much. Because, to be honest, being a digital citizen is also kinda awesome.

These are kids who are not going to be willing to passively sit and be fed information, but who will rather enquire, and create and engage with their world and the people in it. These are kids who are not limited to the circumstances of their surroundings, but rather have the world at their fingertips – literally! They can explore and connect and learn in a way that you could never have imagined. Yes, they are citizens of a digital world that has some dark scary corners, but it is also a world that is expansive and glorious and incredibly beneficial.

Hopefully the advice we've given in the last few chapters will make parents' lives a little easier, and help get kids through their teenage years in one piece. What we really implore parents *not* to do is to lock your child away, banning them from technology and forcing them to hand write letters by the light of a candle. Doing so takes away their ability to communicate and be social; their very lifeblood, and the thing that defines their generation. And because when Little Susie turns 18, emerges from the digital-free cocoon that you've wrapped her in, and gets hold of a smartphone, she's going to get into a whole lot more trouble than if you had just taken the time to educate her when she was young.

Our advice: your kids are digital citizens. You might as well take the time now to teach them responsible digital citizenship.

PART VI

THE LAST BIT

CHAPTER 41

Cutting a long story short

The golden rules for avoiding trouble online

Don't want to read our book? Whatever. We're not mad.

But we still don't want to see you in jail, unemployed or out of pocket for hundreds of thousands of rands. So, if you really want to skip over all the silliness, this is what you need to know:

► Don't film yourself having sex.
► Digital technology and social media are inescapable facts of life. They're not going anywhere.
► The same laws that apply to your conduct in the real world apply to your conduct in cyberspace.
► It doesn't matter if you weren't the one who originally wrote it; if you retweet, share, on-publish or like it, you step into the shoes of a publisher, and you can be held liable for the content.
► The right to freedom of expression is not an unlimited right. It must constantly be balanced against competing rights, such as the right to an unimpaired reputation and the right to dignity.
► Always think about the Five Ps. If you wouldn't want the Police, your Parents, your Principal, a Predator or a Potential employer to see it, don't put it online.
► You construct your own privacy in the digital age. Start to be more vigilant about what you post online.
► Just because it's available online, doesn't mean it's free for the taking.
► Don't be a mean, gross human. Online or offline.
► Be cautious when discussing court proceedings.
► Be careful about divulging confidential information online.
► Don't joke about bombs.
► Criminals operate online. Don't gift them information that will make their job easier.
► The voice on social media is loud. If you own or run a company, make sure that voice is properly managed.
► You can be fired if you breach the duty of good faith that you owe your employer, or if you bring the name of your employer into disrepute

online. Similarly, you can get expelled if you bring the name of your school into disrepute online.

▶ Don't tweet when you're drunk.

▶ Speak to your children about social media. Make sure they understand the risks that come with powerful technology. Implement some device management.

▶ Don't ever think you're anonymous online.

▶ The reputational harm you will suffer by getting it wrong online is potentially far more serious than any legal or disciplinary consequences. So practise reputation management. Every couple of months, google yourself and see if any new mentions have popped up. A helpful tool to keep a tab on your online mentions is to register a Google Alert in your name.

CHAPTER 42

Don't think that calling yourself 'JohnDoe99' will get you off the hook

We still know who you are, and we think your stupid username is stupid

So you've read everything we've had to say, and you get it, but you don't really fancy all this restrictive 'online responsibility' nonsense. So as soon as you finish this book, you're going to go to all your online accounts, delete them and restart your online life as JohnDoe99, changing nothing about the way you conduct yourself.

We hate to be the bearers of bad news, but there is no such thing as anonymity online.

Yes, it is true that most of the social networking sites allow you to use a clever username like JohnDoe99 (Facebook being the notable exception), but even if they don't, there is nothing stopping you from making one up. Yes, it is true that if you read the really, really, *really* fine print governing your use of social media platforms, you'll know that you're supposed to give them your real name when you sign up. But no one checks.

So you are welcome to go forth and become JohnDoe99, but you should always remember that there is a difference between operating under a pseudonym and being truly anonymous. As melodramatic as it sounds, there are ways to find out who you are, and if the circumstances call for it, all will be revealed. Here's how …

The Internet knows everything

Every time you go online, you are assigned something called an Internet Protocol (IP) address. It is like your online ID number, and reveals all sorts of juicy information about where you logged on from and what you did.

Unfortunately for JohnDoe99, technology exists to find out the IP address associated with all content uploaded onto the Internet, and no doubt within the next three months even *more* technology is going to exist to find it out.

Once law enforcement or some other angry person has that information, finding you becomes a whole lot easier.

Take for example Michelle Chapman. Michelle Chapman is a British woman who decided to set up fake Facebook accounts in the name of her father and stepmother, using those accounts to send *herself* numerous messages, including images of child sexual abuse and death threats. Don't ask us why.

She then proceeded to report her father and stepmother to the police. They were subsequently arrested and given a warning. But when forensic enquiries revealed that both accounts had been created from Michelle Chapman's IP address, she found that *she* was the one being arrested. In 2014, she was sentenced to 20 months in prison.

* You might remember that we said upfront that we are not the most technically savvy people in the world, so please pardon us if we oversimplified the whole 'IP address' thing. Yes, we know that if you are dead set on being super creepy and anonymous, there are ways to avoid being traced, but this is a simple book, so let's not get too bogged down in being overly Edward Snowden/James Bond-y, okay?

The websites you use know who you are

Remember that website that you entrusted your personal information to? They can just hand it over to the police. Most websites and online platforms will surrender user information in response to a request from law enforcement. It will require a whole lot of time and money being thrown at the problem, and perhaps one or two flights to California (where many of these technology companies are based), but if the police want to find you, they will.

You're not as clever as you think you are

Chances are you've left some or other clue as to who you are. You get some really clever online snoops who can figure this stuff out pretty quickly.

This was the case in 2013, when the anonymous administrator of a Facebook page called 'UCT Exposed' was tracked down. Originally intended to provide a platform for students at the University of Cape Town to anonymously confess their deepest darkest secrets, it had spiralled out of control, causing serious emotional distress to many of the targets of the confessions that littered the page.

By sending a private message to the administrator of the page, some tech-savvy individuals got him/her to click on a link that enabled them to determine the IP address of the UCT campus computer being used. The whole thing was eventually traced to a particular student, who was confronted with – and denied – the allegations.

Someone could get creative

Whoever wants to know who you are can just *ask*; just send the query out into cyberspace and hope for an answer. Chances are there is someone somewhere who is willing to rat you out. You remember what happened to James. He almost got punched in the head, all because a professional boxer was smart enough to get a little creative.

So our advice: by all means operate under a pseudonym, but never treat that as a licence for you to behave differently to how you would were you operating under your real name. All the tips we've given you in this book, and all the don'ts, will apply equally to you, whether under your real name or as JohnDoe99.

CHAPTER 43

Abracadabra!

Erasing digital you

If this book will have taught you anything, it's that all this digital age and social media stuff is a tricky business! You could lose your job, face public derision and even be thrown in jail for what you say and do online.

So we wouldn't be surprised if you decided that it isn't for you, that it's more stress than it's worth and that you're going back to a simpler time when the only cookies you had to worry about were those delicious things that you ate with tea.

Extricating yourself from a world that is increasingly dependent on 24/7 digital connections is a tough call (we certainly wouldn't advise it), but if you really want to flip the kill switch on Digital You, follow these steps ...

Delete all your online accounts

This includes Facebook, Twitter, LinkedIn, Instagram, Pinterest, any blogs that you may operate, and your Google account (including Gmail). There are cool websites such as JustDelete.me and AccountKiller.com that give step-by-step guidance on how to delete just about every online account you can imagine.

Be aware that deleting your accounts will result in the loss of all content associated with those accounts, so request an archive of your historical activity and download your photos before you click the big red button.

Tell your friends

Removing your accounts doesn't mean that photographs of and information about you won't pop up on other people's accounts. If you're serious about your lack of digital presence, ask your friends to keep content about you off their profile.

Or become a recluse, never leaving the house and never posing for photos. FYI, from personal experience, a good way to ensure that you never leave the house is to write a book ...

Unsubscribe

Unsubscribe from all those electronic mailing lists you were once so drawn to.

Google yourself

If you come across something you want deleted, contact the source directly and ask them to remove the page (or at least, to remove your name). Search engines such as Google, Yahoo and Bing also have mechanisms that allow you to request the complete removal of the associated URL from search results – it won't always work, but you might as well try.

If there is a particular mention that you'd like to bury, and you cannot get it deleted, a useful trick is to completely ignore Step 1 and open as many social media accounts as possible. They don't have to be filled with any information other than your name, and will rank high in online search results. Soon, your unwanted content is pushed onto page 2. And be honest, no one ever really goes onto page 2.

Remove yourself from people databases

Removing your online accounts and search-result mentions is not enough to truly remove yourself from the web, because online databases still store and collect your publicly available information.

It's quite a task to remove yourself from each of these databases, so if you don't have the time, paid services such as DeleteMe will do it for you.

Keep practising online reputation management

Google yourself every so often. And then google yourself from someone else's device. Remember, search engines can *read your mind*, so the results differ depending on the user.

Don't do anything awesome or stupid or otherwise newsworthy

If you do something that warrants media coverage, you'll have a hard time keeping your name off the Internet. So if you'd like to have zero mentions online, banality is the way to do it.

There you go! Go forth and fade into digital oblivion if you so wish. But before you do, we should remind you that it cannot be undone. You will lose your entire online presence – which, for all its risks, also has real value – and you will in all likelihood not be able to restart your accounts in the same name.

If the thought of completely eradicating yourself from cyberspace is a little too drastic for your liking, rather consider adopting a new online persona and new email address for online accounts (although be aware that some websites prohibit the use of false information). Most importantly, this will not make you anonymous or put you beyond the reach of law enforcement (see Chapter 42), but it is a good first step in dissociating your online self from your real-world self.

What to do if you're a victim

Taking back control online

Now that you know all about the various legal remedies available to you if you are the victim of online impropriety, it's time to put that knowledge into action. Because if you *do* find yourself faced with what you consider to be unlawful online conduct, it's not enough to feel outraged and shout about how you're fairly certain that you are the target of something or other which that *Don't Film Yourself Having Sex* book says was wrong.

You actually have to do something about it.

Step 1: Take screenshots
As soon as you make an allegation of wrongfulness, the perpetrator is going to delete the evidence. So think ahead by taking screenshots and keeping a log of all communications.

Step 2: Take notes
Keep notes of as much identifying information as possible, including the offender's screen name, email address and ISP.

Step 3: Don't feed the trolls
As much as you want to respond to or engage directly with online baddies, just don't. If you feel it necessary to defend yourself or your company against scurrilous allegations, feel free to issue a statement acknowledging the content and denying it in the strongest terms. But don't link to it. That will only fuel the fire.

Step 4: Block
In the case of a cyberbully or online predator, immediately block the user and/or stop logging into the website where the harm occurred.

Step 5: Make some changes
If the impropriety continues, change your online information or delete your account.

Step 6: Report to website
Most social media platforms allow users to report users that breach the terms and conditions of the website. You may also report specific content that you deem to be in violation of your rights. These are useful tools and you shouldn't be afraid to use them.

Step 7: Report to ISP
Once notified, ISPs may be held to be legally liable for the content hosted on their pages. Reporting illegal content to your and the website's ISP is a good way to get it deleted.

Step 8: Get legal advice and report to authorities
If you think that you are the victim of a crime, contact the authorities.

Step 9: Make sure
Always remember that everyone has a right of free speech, so only take action if you think that this right is being abused to the extent that it amounts to a violation of your rights and/or a criminal act. If you are unsure, rather consult a lawyer. The law frowns upon vexatious attempts to have objectionable content removed, and if you go around reporting perfectly acceptable behaviour and bullying companies or individuals into removing content, you could be the one that finds yourself in trouble.

How to lose a friend in 10 ways:
The most annoying habits of the social media generation

1. *#blessed*.

2. **Telling your significant other how much you love them/how lucky you are to have them.** Tell them to their face. They're probably sitting right next to you.

3. **Posting pictures of your uterus.** We get it. You're excited about your pregnancy. But to the rest of us, that is just a picture of your insides. Gross.

4. **Retweeting compliments.** Well done, people think you're awesome. We don't.

5. **Engagement photo shoot/maternity photo shoot.** We know, we know. You're *#blessed*, and you look great with all that soft lighting, but stop it. It makes you look like a jackass.

6. **Checking in at the gym.** Doing exercise is not an achievement. Unless you're us.

7. **Birth shots.** Only you think your baby is cute when it's covered in afterbirth. Please wrap the little munchkin up in a blanket, wait until your wife has recovered,

---

and *only then* do the inevitable 'Welcome to the world' announcement.

8. **'Why does this always happen to me?'**
   'What's wrong hun?'
   'Never mind. I don't want to talk about it.'
   No, no, NO!

9. **Checking in at the Business Class lounge of the airport.** Noted. You're a tool.

10. **'Can't wait for the weekend! #Friday #colourfulsocks #suitandtie #hardworkpaysoff #dinner #drinks #friends #party #jozi #lovemylife #yolo**
    #gonnapunchyouintheface

CHAPTER 45

What next?

The future of digital technology and the law

'The law has to take into account changing realities not only tech-nologically but also socially or else it will lose credibility in the eyes of the people. Without credibility, law loses legitimacy. If law loses legitimacy, it loses acceptance. If it loses acceptance, it loses obe-dience. It is imperative that the courts respond appropriately to changing times, acting cautiously and with wisdom.'
– *Judge Willis,* H v W 2013 (2) SA 530 GSJ

Let's do a little experiment ...
Raise your hand if you think that you should be arrested on terrorism charges if you tweet 'Crap! The airport is closed. You've got a week and a bit to get your shit together otherwise I'm blowing the airport sky high!!'
Raise your hand if you think that a 17-year-old boy should be convicted for the creation of child pornography for taking a picture of himself naked and sending it to his 17-year-old girlfriend (with whom he is engaged in an entirely lawful sexual relationship).
Raise your hand if you think you should be found guilty of defamation for putting a status on Facebook that says, 'Penalty? Are you kidding me? This ref is fucking crazy!'
Anyone? *Anyone?*

We're guessing that not many of you raised a hand (not least because this is a fictitious experiment, and if you *did* randomly raise your hand while quietly reading a book, people may begin to question whether *you* are in fact 'fucking crazy').
But our little made-up experiment helps illustrate a very important point ...
We've told you that, as far as the letter of the law is concerned, com-munications made over social media can and do fall within the remit of various offences, as well as give rise to a range of different civil claims.
Yet that doesn't change the fact that the stringent application of 20th-century laws to 21st-century behaviour is increasingly controversial, and

there is growing sympathy for those who have had the full might of the law come down on them on the basis of their social media mistakes. It has also given rise to two major concerns.

Firstly, it appears to stand in direct opposition with how people *actually* understand and experience online communications, namely as a distinct variety of speech that differs from offline speech and warrants unique treatment by the law.

By shoehorning digital behaviours into existing legal categories that do not align with the general public's understanding of how they should be treated, the law loses legitimacy in the eyes of those it is trying to regulate. And once it loses legitimacy, it leaves people feeling threatened and suspicious of intervention.

Secondly, the overly strict regulation of social media communications has the potential to undo a lot of good. What we must not forget is that, at its heart, social media encourages the exercise of freedom of expression – and that's a good thing. By being too restrictive, there is a risk that users will overcompensate and feel discouraged from speaking freely. All of a sudden, people may decide not to express their opinion on something, for fear of landing up in jail, being sued or losing their job.

Given the nuances of online communications, by-the-letter application of the law and other regulatory codes is sometimes a blunt instrument with which to strike the correct balance between rights of free speech and conflicting rights to privacy, dignity, reputation and to be protected from harassment.

On this basis, we are strong proponents of rethinking the regulation of social media communications, in order to get the delicate but important balance that is required to be struck between free speech and conflicting rights *just right*. Like Goldilocks!

In our view, regulators (prosecutors, judges and employers) need to acknowledge that social media is not going anywhere anytime soon and that social media communications represent a modern, unique and distinct type of speech that should not always be brought within the four corners of expansive 20th-century rules. A new legal and regulatory framework must be devised that is at the very least alive to the nuances and complexities of the digital era and online speech, by providing a subjective element to the free speech balance – particularly the significance of context and tone of social media communications, the intention of the speaker, the perception of the audience and the widespread use of hyperbole. By incorporating these elements into regulation, and higher levels of speech tolerance, the scales will be rebalanced in a manner that suits the intricacies of social media communications.

Obviously we are not talking about clearly harmful and objectionable content – that which is intended to incite violence, constitutes threats of harm, is unacceptably intolerant or derogatory, amounts to a serious crime or unacceptable violation of the rights or others, or constitutes the sexual exploitation of a child – in which instances the perpetrator must of course face the legal consequences. We are instead talking about those succinct, impromptu, often flippant communications that are so typical of one-to-many online conversations, or the innocent use of technology

186

by teenagers who don't know any better: the 'jokes' that fall flat, the innocent stream-of-consciousness-type speech, the off-the-cuff remarks within a limited social circle, and consensual sexting.

Let's look to the UK ... At one point, there were reports that there were an average of *three* social media-based arrests being made every day, for offences ranging from hoax threats to harassment of ex-partners. In recognition of this absurdity, the Crown Prosecution Service (CPS) issued a set of guidelines aimed at striking the correct balance between freedom of expression and the need to uphold criminal law.

As explained by the incumbent Director of Public Prosecutions, while credible threats of violence and targeted campaigns of harassment should be prosecuted, there must be a high threshold of intervention into social media communications that are merely offensive, shocking, disturbing or distasteful, the prosecution of which will in many cases be unlikely to be in the public interest.

As more and more people get into trouble for what they say online, similar guidelines from the National Prosecuting Authority would be welcomed. In particular, we would hope that the NPA accepts a high threshold for intervention into social media communications, taking heed of the CPS Guidelines' acknowledgement of the importance of context, as well as the subjective intention of the speaker. Furthermore, prosecution should be avoided where genuine remorse is shown and the communication is quickly removed. In terms of civil law, we too hope that the courts and judges take similar concerns on board in formulating their judgments.

There you go. Those are our two cents.

CHAPTER 46

Conclusion

You live in the digital age. Computers, the Internet, social media: all these things are an inescapable fact of life for you.

However, having read this book, you might be wishing this wasn't so. You might be wishing that you were born in an age where tweeting was done by birds, googling was done by babies, and the only technology you had to worry about was your microwave.

But how boring!

Isn't it fantastic that we get to live in a world where everyone has a platform to make themselves heard, unconstrained by geographical boundaries; where we can share and create and interact and collaborate; and where we can revolutionise the world for good at the click of a button? Web 2.0 affords us *freedom*: freedom from the constraints of the real world, freedom to do and say more, and freedom of choice.

And who doesn't love freedom?

We suppose, however, that you're wondering what use all of that freedom is if you're going to end up in jail, being sued, or losing your job and reputation. Is the risk really worth the reward?

Well, yes. Yes, it is.

We know we've scared you. In fact, we *hope* we've scared you. But we're really just playing Bad Cop. The Good Cop in us actually champions digital technology. We want you to exercise the voice that social media gives you. We want you to take the opportunity to expand social participation. We want you to reap all the extraordinary benefits of this life-changing technology.

But we just want you to do so responsibly. We don't want you to get it wrong. And we don't want you to film yourself having sex.

Further resources

The world of social media moves so fast, and what we've said in this book is constantly changing. To make sure you're up to date, here are some further resources:

Twitter
The hashtags #smlaw and #socialmedialaw are a good place to start.

People to follow on Twitter
We tweet updates as they happen, so follow us:
@EmmaSadleir
@TamsynDeBeer

Other South African social media law tweeters
@Dariomilo
Media and information lawyer and partner at Webber Wentzel. Dario is Emma's mentor and also blogs at www.dariomilo.com.

@pauljacobson
Founder of WebTechLaw. While you're at it, follow @webtechlaw on Twitter as well. Paul also blogs at http://webtechlaw.com/posts.

@nickhallsa
Lawyer at Michalsons, gamer, board gamer and general geek.

@_SocialMediaLaw
Attorneys at Bowman Gilfillan with an interest in social media law.

International legal tweeters
There are so many but here are some of the best:

@podlegal
Jamie White. One of our favourites. Solicitor Director and Owner of Pod Legal. Excellent updates from Australia and New Zealand.

@meejalaw
Legal discussion and news for online publishers gathered by @jtownend.

@SMediaLaw
Commentary, news and analysis at the intersection of social media and the law. Updates by leading tech and media lawyers.

@SocialMediaLaw1 and @UKSocialMedia
Social media law updates from Glen Gilmore – one of *Forbes'* 'Top 50 Social Media Power Influencers' and 'Top 50 Social Media Bloggers'.

@MarkLewisLawyer
English media lawyer living in Los Angeles – focus on media, defamation and privacy.

@socialmedia_law
Social media: corporate social media, law and strategy; social media risks and tips.

@ScottMalouf
An attorney helping attorneys use social media, text and email evidence.

@hansflensted
Cool Dane, social lawyer, happy cyclist. Expect social media and legal stuff.

@internetcases
Attorney: copyright, trademark, software, Internet, new media.

@igrande
NYS Bar Social Media Committee Co-Chair; Sr. E-Discovery Attorney, Hughes Hubbard; Adjunct Professor, St John's Law School.

International social media tweeters

@TweetSmarter
Excellent tips, tools, Twitter news and tech support.

@mashsocialmedia
The latest in social media, plus tips on Twitter, Facebook, Pinterest, Google+, Vine, Foursquare and more from @Mashable. Website: mashable.com/social media/.

@fieldhousemedia
Social media company that assists students in looking after their online CVs. Education, monitoring and strategy.

@DionneLew
Social media strategist and CEO of The Social Executive.

@SocialAssurity
Social Assurity empowers students with insight on how college admissions and prospective employers assess social media activities in their acceptance decisions.

Blogs

http://inforrm.wordpress.com/
The International Forum for Responsible Media (Inforrm for short) was set up to debate issues of media responsibility. You can sign up to their excellent newsletter.

http://journlaw.com/
The blog of Mark Pearson PhD – journalist, professor, media law and ethics researcher, teacher and author of *Blogging and Tweeting Without Getting Sued – A Global Guide to the Law for Anyone Writing Online* (Allen & Unwin, 2012). Tweets from the handle @JournLaw.

http://ipkkat.com/
Predominantly news on intellectual property. Since June 2003 the IPKat weblog has covered copyright, patent, trademark, info-tech and privacy/confidentiality issues from a mainly UK and European perspective.

http://theitlawyer.blogspot.com/
Andrew Murray – Professor of Law at the London School of Economics and author of *Information Technology Law: The Law and Society* (Oxford University Press, 2013). Taught both Tamsyn and Emma. Tweets from the handle @AndrewDMurray.

http://bloglawonline.blogspot.com/
The blog of Eric P. Robinson, an attorney and scholar, focusing on legal issues involving the media, including the Internet and social media.

http://mslods.com/
Lawyer and academic – provides comprehensive global law and technology round-ups from Australia.

Online safety tools

http://www.cellphonesafety.co.za/
Gives step-by-step instructions to make your child's phone and tablet safer. You can also join the newsletter for updates.

http://cybercrime.org.za/local-resources/
A list of websites publishing cybercrime and related Internet safety information that can assist South African users.

http://www.business.ftc.gov/privacy-and-security/childrens-privacy
Federal Trade Commission's Children's Online Privacy.

www.getnetwise.org
The GetNetWise website is a comprehensive resource for parents, sponsored by Internet industry companies and public-interest organisations.

www.connectsafely.org
ConnectSafely is a resource for parents, teens and experts to discuss safe socialising on the web and mobile devices.

http://safely.yahoo.com/parents/
Yahoo's online safety guide provides a section for parents.

www.netfamilynews.org
Net Family News is an Internet safety-oriented blog.

Acknowledgements

We're not quite sure how, but we managed to put this book together in a very short period of time. Now it's all a bit of a blur, but we're fairly certain that we weren't much fun to be around during what was a rollercoaster few months. Suffice to say it all involved unprecedented levels of hibernation, sleepless nights (make that weeks), very many days in pyjamas and a lot of coffee.

For those who had to endure the general aura of panic that surrounded us during this time – thank you. Jenny, Philip, Michelle, Kirstin, Frank, little Nano and the Bees; Gerry Baby, The Shirlinator, Naughty Nick and the Lawyer Barbies; our very patient roomie Plant; Big Daddy and Louis; and every other friend and family member that crossed our path: we (literally) couldn't have done it without your support and encouragement. You are all legends and we love you.

But before we even got to the stage of hysterically writing the book, there were people that were fundamental to our legal education, and we emerge from the haze of writing conscious of how indebted we are to them. First and foremost, we both had the privilege of studying under some of the leading minds in the field of information technology and media law at the London School of Economics; thanks to scholarships awarded by the *Oppenheimer Memorial Trust* and *The Skye International Foundation Trust*. To Andrew Murray, Andrew Scott, Dev Gangjee, Anne Barron and Orla Lynskey: your teachings, guidance and support were invaluable, and we owe much of our success to the knowledge and confidence that came from our time at the LSE. We also need to acknowledge our friends and fellow students at the LSE, from whom we learned so much and who have come to form part of a treasured network of friends and colleagues. It was cold, it rained a lot, but it was a hell of a lot of fun and the best year of our lives! Lastly, our formative years at Webber Wentzel were enormously valuable in providing the legal foundation that we needed to write this book, and we must thank all we worked with during our time at the firm for their mentorship. On behalf of Emma in particular, massive thanks and gratitude to Dario Milo, mentor and friend.